RESTORED

TOM HARDIMAN

FOREWORD BY RICK JOYNER

MorningStar Publications
www.MorningStarMinistries.org

Restored
By Tom Hardiman

©2023 Tom Hardiman
First printing, 2023
All rights reserved.

Distributed by MorningStar Publications, Inc.,
a division of MorningStar Fellowship Church
375 Star Light Drive, Fort Mill, SC 29715

www.MorningStarMinistries.org
1-800-542-0278

Cover: Esther Jun
Layout: Rebecca Lambertsen

ISBN: 978-1-60708-708-3

For a free catalog of MorningStar resources, please call 1-800-542-0278

About the Cover

The church pictured on the cover, known as *Frauen-kirche*, or Church of Our Lady, in Dresden, Germany was originally built between 1726 and 1743. Prior to World War II, Dresden was known as "The Florence on the Elbe" and considered one of the world's most beautiful cities due to its architecture and art treasures.

However, World War II brought terrible suffering and devastation to much of Europe when Dresden became the focal point of merciless Allied retaliation. On February 13, 1945, Dresden was bombed, and the entire city center was destroyed, including *Frauenkirche*.

After the war, Dresden and East Germany came under communist rule. Attempts were made to restore the church, yet she remained in ruins for nearly fifty years, until after the Iron Curtain collapsed in 1989.

In the faded upper background of the cover is an image of *Frauenkirche* in ruins. Forty-eight years after its destruction, the meticulous process of restoration began. Great care was given to carefully mark and number every stone which could be used in the rebuilding process. In all, 91,500 stones were identified for reuse, and 8,390 of the blackened, burnt stones became part of the building's façade, just as in the rebuilding of God's temple (see Nehemiah 4:2). Both new and burnt stones were used in the reconstruction of the church, which can clearly be seen on the outside of the structure. The rebuilding of the exterior and interior took more than eleven years. Finally completed in 2005, this former wreckage became a new and glorious structure.

The prophetic message of this cover speaks volumes. Many in the body of Christ today have suffered significant failure and devastation. Many feel lost and forsaken in the debris that surrounds their lives. Then, after what may seem like a lifetime, the rebuilding process can begin.

Likewise, God has stationed us at MorningStar Ministries in a facility formerly known as PTL's Heritage USA. This site was once known worldwide as a place of shame, mockery, and contempt. However, under Rick Joyner's guidance, God has seen fit to restore and rebuild this facility. Today, MorningStar has also become a prophetic beacon of hope for restoration and destiny. As you read this book, I trust that God, who restores all things, will become your close companion on your journey to restoration!

Endorsements

Tom Hardiman has written an incredible book; it is instructive, encouraging, and affirming. The book follows the struggles we all face and how God has a plan for our lives, even when we cannot readily see it. Through his story of betrayal by people whom he trusted and thought were his friends, Tom shares how he had to lean on God as his life spun out of control. He then watched as God put his life back together. Today, because of his experiences, Tom can mentor many people, including me. I am blessed to have him in my life.

—*LTG (R) Jerry Boykin, Executive Vice President, Family Research Council*

It is a joy and honor to recommend this book to you. I have known Tom and his family for many years. They are precious and upright. Within this book, you will discover that Almighty God is always with us and working all things out for His glory and for our good. You will be greatly encouraged and helped to see that, even in hard times, you are never forsaken. You will be encouraged to stay focused and never give up because you are chosen by God.

—*Bobby Conner, Founder, Eagles View Ministries*

Seldom is there an individual I know closely enough to make my highest recommendation. Tom Hardiman is one of those individuals. Tom and I have worked closely for the past fourteen years. He is a man of exceptional devotion to Christ and truly a leader among leaders. He has spent most of the last fifteen years devoted to helping others succeed in ministry. His book, *Restored*, outlines his journey, which he uses as a backdrop for powerful life and spiritual lessons. His vulnerability and transparency as he discusses his journey are remarkable. I recommend this to anyone struggling to see how the seeming disappointments in our lives can be rebuilt to form a life mission.

—*Dave Yarnes, Executive Vice President, MorningStar Ministries*

Over the many years I have known Tom Hardiman, I have always respected his sense of loyalty and commitment. Now, after reading his book, I understand much more fully those qualities which have been engrafted into his character. Like so many leaders throughout biblical and church history, we travel through various peaks and valleys in our journeys with the Lord to bring us to the place of our ultimate destiny. I love the transparency by which Tom shares those various junctures in his life, from great disappointments to notable achievements, all wrought by the grace of God. I believe this book will be a great encouragement to those who read it.

—*Paul Keith Davis, Founder, White Dove Ministries*

Some men write books, and other men share their lives. The book you hold in your hand was written by a man who has seen both sides of the Jordan. No matter where you stand in life, this book has something to teach and encourage you. From his life as an Olympic athlete, to the mental ward of a major hospital, to a major leader of an international ministry, Tom weaves the stories of his life in a masterful way. *Restored* is not only the title of this book but also his life story. His faithful wife, Mary Anne, also shares the ups and down she faced as a wife caught in the whirlwind of it all. This book is filled with scriptural insights from two people who, together, came through the battle stronger in love and in spirit. This book is a divine appointment to encourage you wherever you stand in life! When you finish, you will be filled with new hope. You will be encouraged with new strength to remain at the wheel and finish your God-given assignment!

—*Dr. Andrew Surace, Pastor, Christ Fellowship Church, Marmora, New Jersey*

Restored is a must-read for every wounded warrior in ministry who needs hope. To quote Tom, "Rocky roads, contradictory circumstances, disillusionment, despair—God uses all these things to prepare great leaders for great purposes." If you need hope that God can still use you, or that God has a purpose for all you are going through or have gone through, please take the time to read *Restored*. You'll be glad you did!

—*Donna Hoover, Pastor, Abide in the Vine Fellowship, Owego, New York*

If you have ever struggled with delays, betrayals, or the pain of watching dreams shatter in your life and ministry, this book will lift you up. It is a powerful reminder of the hidden hand of God shaping His servants for their destiny. Tom has written an inspirational book that deals with the gritty reality of everyday ministry and its many challenges and disappointments. While his journey reveals the pain of his own experience, it releases abundant healing and hope to everyone who has struggled over the veiled ways God prepares His leaders. Tom has pulled back the veil to help us see the hand of God as He guides us to victory. This is an important book for everyone in ministry, and all who aspire to be significantly used by God.

—*Randal Cutter, Pastor, New Dawn Community Church, Coral Springs, Florida*

With a fresh approach to the age-old tale of betrayal and heartache, *Restored* takes you from heartbreak to rejoicing. Littered with nuggets of wisdom from a life of ministry and study of the Word, *Restored* shares insights that are easily applied and will melt away any lingering bitterness and confusion that follows a traumatic event. Tom Hardiman shares how to turn tragedy and heartache into a fertile field for God to plant something new and fulfilling. Anyone who has suffered loss or betrayal will find renewed hope and wholeness. *Restored* is a roadmap to victory with lifelong keys for effective spiritual warfare.

—*Tracy Schellhorn, Director of MFM Intercessory Network, Manifest Ministries, WingSpan Prayer Network*

Acknowledgements

First, I would like to thank Rick Joyner for all the work he has done over the years, both seen and unseen, to establish MorningStar Ministries. Under Rick's leadership, he has created an atmosphere to restore and rebuild God's people, even when those actions have been costly to him. His counsel to me and my family during our years of distress were critical. Without Rick, this story would not have been written.

I would also like to thank:

Nathalie Seguin, who played an instrumental role in helping organize my notes which eventually went into this manuscript, developed a suggested timeline for chapters, and offered insights on the overall management of this project.

Trevor Tiessen, who has been a loyal and faithful support to MorningStar, to our MFM Office, and to me personally. At key times, Trevor has helped lift the pastoral weight and take care of the MFM members. My confidence in his ability to assist with complex issues has enabled me to focus on the completion of this book.

Deb Williams, for the encouragement I received from her during the early stages of this book, which became the incentive for me to press on. It was a project worth completing!

Jeff Oliver, who read through the first manuscript and consistently told me this was a story that needed to be written. His words of encouragement were timely. Jeff is now our Publications Managing Editor.

Our editing staff here at MorningStar, who, from start to finish, are amazing people who help fulfill MorningStar's mandate to produce "meat in due season."

Esther Jun, the graphic designer who produced the front cover of this book. The cover tells the whole story!

Anne Baron for helping push this book across the finish line. Anne is contributing significantly to MorningStar in this hour.

My wonderful children who, by the grace of God, love and serve the Lord, with their spouses and our seven wonderful grandkids. Periodically I mention my children and the profound lessons we learned together. I value their contribution to this story as we journeyed our way through these years. I am most proud of the love, grace, and wisdom they have shared and the blessing they have been to my life.

My wife, Mary Anne's, contributions to this book are at least twofold. Through our dark days, Mary Anne's tenacious persistence to see the will of God done in our family's life was key to this story being written. Her refusal to yield any more ground to the enemy and her words of encouragement and timely counsel kept us afloat. The first word Bob Jones gave to Mary Anne was to identify the Spirit of counsel and might which rested upon her. We certainly drew upon that gift throughout our ordeal.

My wife's second contribution was her skill in editing this book, and her handiwork can be seen in every chapter. Through her editing process, she rearranged important thoughts I had written and skillfully and artfully weaved them into the storyline. Time and again, she made suggestions on how to approach the next phase of the book. Her contributions were invaluable.

Over the years, God has built us into a team, and together, as this book reveals, we have climbed our way out of some deep and hurtful places. Indeed, two are better than one!

Finally, and most importantly, I thank the Lord Jesus, my Redeemer and Restorer! He is the unseen hand to which glory belongs. There was a day in my life when He made the determination there would be no more loss, and the restoration process began. It is He who restores lost years, lost hopes, and lost dreams. He is the One who turns ashes into beauty and makes all things new. To Him be glory and power, forever and ever. May His kingdom come!

Table *of* Contents

Foreword

As a friend once told us, "The favor of God is worth a lifetime of effort." This book is about how to attract God's favor to our lives. It is a story that many have lived in their own way and for the same purpose, so they could be used by God for His ultimate purpose in this age—to help lead all who will come to the redemption, healing, and restoration of all they were created to be.

Tom and Mary Anne Hardiman are two of the longest-serving members of the MorningStar leadership team and have helped build this ministry into what it is today. They both have remarkable gifts for extracting key insights from the Scriptures and current events and applying them to what God is doing today. They have not only been pillars to help keep us stable and on course, but they have also been builders whose words and messages have been key in making MorningStar what it has become.

The true Christian life is the most exciting and fulfilling life we can live on this earth. It is also the most difficult. Though this is shocking to some popular modern doctrines, the Christian's life is meant to be difficult. This life is training for those who are called to reign with Him in the age to come. We learn in this life that we cannot have a victory without a battle, and we cannot have a big victory without a *big* battle. The Lord called Himself "a Warrior," and He called us to be like Him. We are here to learn to fight, but without carnal weapons and without hurting people. We are here to heal.

I have watched Tom and Mary Anne go through some big battles and win. Their stories will help us do the same.

The saying is true: if we have a Saul in our lives, God must see a David in us. Saul was brutal, unjust, and driven by jealousy to attack those with great purpose, but attacks like his only fashion us into what God wants us to be. David would not have been the great king he became were it not for the training he received through Saul's abuse.

As difficult as this was for David in his formative years, it was worse for "the Son of David," Jesus. No one has, or ever will be more unjustly treated than Jesus. He was not only without sin, but He also went about doing good, healing, and setting people free. He did so only after making the unfathomable sacrifice of emptying Himself of His divine nature to become like us. Then He was executed by the very ones for whom He had done this, and by the cruelest torture of the time. He not only forgave those who did this to Him, but He also asked the Father to forgive them.

At times I have worked very hard to forgive people, believing that if I did, God would judge them! Jesus did not want the Father to do this. He fully paid the price for what we did to both Him and the Father through our sin and rebellion.

The Father so loved us that He sent His beloved Son to do this. Neither of them wanted us to pay the price for our transgressions. Instead, they wanted us to receive forgiveness and recover from the damage we had done to ourselves. Jesus told us what would fully restore us: if we forgave and loved each other with the same love with which He loved us.

King David not only forgave Saul, but he also honored him even after Saul died. David took care of his children, let them eat at his own table, and defended them against anyone who threatened them. This was the opposite of what kings did in those days. When one assumed a throne, the first thing they did was seek out heirs of the previous king to kill them, so they would not become a threat. David was of a "different spirit."

It was this heart that compelled the Lord to say, **"David is a man after My own heart" (see Acts 13:22).** Jesus, the "Son of David," likewise demonstrated this heart on the cross. For this, God established for David a throne that would last forever, which Jesus, the Son of David, is now seated upon. If we want our work to last, our ability to forgive will be our most important characteristic. Only what God does through us will last, and we will always find forgiveness central to who He is and what He is doing.

The degree to which we can forgive others is a barometer of our true spiritual maturity. It is the surest sign that we are living by the two greatest commandments—to love God and to love one another as He loved us. For this reason, we should see every time we are unjustly treated as an opportunity to grow in this most important grace we must have in service to our King.

I have watched Tom and Mary Anne go through some of the most difficult trials imaginable—some of which are recorded in these pages—but they became better, not bitter. Though I have heard them recount what happened, I have never heard them do so with bitterness or resentment. I watched them get healed, and once they were healed, they became healers.

It is worth noting that the second temple, the one which had been restored after the destruction of the first, was built with "burnt stones." This temple the Lord promised would have a "greater glory" than the first. Many people have missed their callings because they were hurt in the church and left. If we have not been burned, we are not qualified to be part of the church of greater glory. Getting hurt and burned is an opportunity to grow and take our place among those who will be His eternal dwelling place. However, only the wise seize such opportunities.

We must not waste these trials of being treated unfairly, but instead see them as great opportunities to grow in love by growing in the greatest demonstration of love—forgiveness. For this reason, when the apostle Paul had his apostolic authority challenged, he did not recount all the great things he had done or churches he had raised up. Instead, he recounted his afflictions. It is not the great vision we have or great things we have done that determines the authority with which the Lord can entrust us. It is how we handle our afflictions.

For us to truly follow Christ, one major issue must be settled: we are not who we are because of our experiences or environment, but because of how we *react* to our experiences and environment. This is what the Lord told Cain to preempt what he would do to his brother (see Genesis 4:7). Cain did not listen, and the terrible history of evil we do to each other began. Jesus came to change this, but first He called those who would follow Him to become different like Him.

We are healed by Jesus' stripes. Where He was wounded, He received authority to heal us. The same is true with us. For every wound we receive, we receive authority to heal others of similar wounds. The key is, we must be healed before we can be healers, and we are healed by forgiving.

James said, **"Count it all joy when you fall into various trials" (see James 1:2)**, and Peter wrote, the **"trials of your faith"** are **"much more precious than gold" (see I Peter 1:6-7)**. This means when we encounter various trials, we should get more excited than if we had found a bag of gold! Those who walk in spiritual and eternal realities will get excited. Those who are still trapped in the temporary life will not.

Certainly, my trust in Tom and Mary Anne grew as I watched how they navigated through their difficulties, but especially how their faith grew in them. What they went through with their granddaughter, Sloane, had to have been much more difficult than what they went through with the church in New Jersey. They shared their trials with us, asking us to pray for Sloane, her parents, and for them, but I never heard them complain. When they talked about it, they exuded faith, not self-pity, despite the seeming impossibilities. Obviously, God also took note because they saw miracle after miracle.

Still, their lives are remarkable, not just by how they navigated through trials, which reveals their true character, but through their impressive devotion to building and healing others. They have done this with a sword in one hand and a trowel in the other. While fighting their own battles, they were building others. Only in eternity will we know how much they have accomplished, but I know MorningStar would not be where it is or what it is without them. I know many others who would say the same thing.

In Isaiah 40, we are told to prepare for the coming of the Lord by building a highway. That "highway" is God's "higher way." We are here to work on this highway upon which the kingdom of God will come. This book explains much about how this is done.

—*Rick Joyner*

"In this you greatly rejoice,
though now for a little while,
if need be, you have been grieved
by various trials,

that the genuineness of your
faith, being much more
precious than gold
that perishes,
though it is tested by fire,
may be found to praise,
honor, and glory at the
revelation of Jesus Christ"

I Peter 1:6-7

1

Forsaken

It was the worst day of my life. On January 8, 1991, I was in an elevator on the way to the eighth floor of St. Francis Hospital in Trenton, New Jersey.

I knew this hospital well. I knew every staircase and shortcut. When I was a kid I delivered newspapers to this hospital six days a week for six years, yet in all that time I had never been to the eighth floor. This was the psychiatric ward where the patients were held under lock and key and where unauthorized personnel were not permitted.

As a paperboy, I heard horror stories of what happened on the eighth floor. Now I was about to be admitted as a patient to that frightening place. How did my life ever come to this? I could never have imagined this being a reality for me, but after the elevator door slid open, the attendant unlocked the door to the ward and then locked it again behind us. I was now a patient in the psych ward. This truly was "the worst day of my life."

Something seemed broken inside. I had been experiencing panic attacks and was under a significant amount of stress and anxiety. Sadly, I had come from three days of meetings with the supervising leaders of our church movement. At the end of the three days, the leaders asked me to resign as pastor of the church I had planted thirteen years prior. The leaders had determined that I had become a danger to my church and to its people. If I did not resign, their apostolic covering would be removed from the church. I had been taught that this lack of endorsement would result in grave consequences for me, my family, and my future.

Over the years I grew to respect and love the leaders of our movement. The weight of their words was crushing. Though I did not agree with their evaluation, this devastating recommendation was like a death sentence. In the back of my mind, I had considered that a religious or political spirit might be at work, but the size of this network and my respect for them did not permit me to entertain such a conclusion. As I climbed into bed, I was given doses of antidepressants. I felt overwhelmed by the decision that lay before me, but honestly, for the first time in a long time, I felt safe and locked away from the voices of criticism.

This was not my first review with these overseers. Eighteen months earlier, a similar set of meetings covered the same ground. That meeting began at 9:00 a.m. and ended at 4:30 a.m. the following morning. In that meeting, all the major decisions I had made over the first thirteen years of my ministry were reviewed, and their conclusion was that I was not at fault. Nevertheless, the grueling nature of that meeting had a lasting impact on my soul and forever fractured my trust in the leadership of this movement.

Adding to this tension was the fact that my chief accuser was the son-in-law of our head apostle. At one point, my chief accuser had been my closest friend, but over the years, as I drifted from the traditions of the movement, our relationship became strained, and eventually I was labeled "disloyal" to the apostle.

After my first review, it was decided a change was needed to create a more peaceful environment. The son-in-law would return to headquarters, and from there my eventual replacement would be sent to assist me. In the short term, this sounded like a reasonable solution. However, eventually my replacement's leadership proved to be more toxic than our original arrangement of him just assisting me.

The reviews of my ministry style were largely focused on my autocratic style of leadership, the pace at which I led the church, and my overbearing nature. Some of these accusations were true, and while I had attempted to correct these ministry flaws, the underlying issue was my gradual departure from the practices and traditions of our movement.

Our movement overregulated our reach into people's lives. Some traditions included no dating for teenagers, no makeup for teenage girls, and a host of other overly burdensome requirements. Such issues reached a boiling point in our K-12 school. At one point, our church was divided over whether we should permit teenage dating. I was convinced the Lord was directing us to end such legalistic practices. It was on these grounds a battle was fought that culminated in the recommendation that I resign.

If I were to evaluate my personal temperament, I would not consider myself a weak man. On the contrary, I had accomplished much in forty years. I had earned a full basketball scholarship to an NCAA Division 1 college in the Northeastern U.S. I had earned an award as a distinguished military graduate, and I had found myself among an elite company of athletes representing the USA as a Team Handball player in the 1972 Munich Olympics and again in the 1974 World Cup in Berlin.

I was saved in 1973, then attended and graduated from a school of ministry in Anchorage, Alaska. Then I returned to my hometown and planted a church. The church quickly grew into a thriving work with a full-time K-12 Christian school, a ministry school of eighty students, and a local church of more than three hundred. One does not accomplish all this without an abundance of God's grace and a considerable amount of grit and determination. However, as I lay in that hospital bed, I was only a shadow of my former self. Broken and confused, I had lost hope that even God could help and had numerous perplexing questions.

We began our church with nothing but a vision from God. We planted the church in 1978 with no money and no support or pledges from the people who stood with us. So, week by week, month by month, year by year, we continued to put feet to the vision, and the work grew. God brought key people to help us build and opened doors for us to purchase a former theater, which we converted into a beautiful church. The purchase of that building alone was supernatural.

We rented office space from a realtor. His wife, who was not a believer, had a dream that we purchased the theater for $90,000. The building was worth at least twice that, but we did in fact purchase it for that exact figure. At our building dedication, two elderly women, who were first-time visitors, shared an amazing testimony. Thirty-seven years prior, the two had walked around that building seven times and claimed it for God's use. They shared how God had spoken to them and said He would use the building as a place to demonstrate His glory. They came to the building dedication to share the fulfillment of God's promise. This was surefire confirmation that God was with us.

Over the years, our church grew to more than three hundred members, and we completed and paid for two major building projects. Our bank accounts were thriving, and the once dilapidated building was within a few thousand dollars of being debt-free. As I pondered resigning, I asked the following questions: "Was God still with us?" "What was the future of the K-12 Christian school with seventy students?" "What would happen to our ministry school of eighty students?" "Was all this to be surrendered?"

Nevertheless, a pitched battle was fought, and the leader of our movement wanted me removed. This leader was actively soliciting support from my elders and eventually convinced them I must leave. Leaders whom I once considered close friends surprised me as they participated in this feeding frenzy of criticisms, all aimed at me.

As I considered resigning, I could not imagine returning to such a field of battle. So, from my hospital bed on the eighth floor of St. Francis Hospital, with great sadness, I officially resigned as pastor of the church. Thirteen years of labor, sacrifice, and hard work required to build a work of God was gone with a simple signature on a piece of paper—gone!

I had no idea what lay before me. How would I take care of my wife and three children? Exhausted, depleted, alone, and in a cloud of failure, I resigned. Worst of all, I concluded I had failed God. This truly was "the worst day of my life!"

"These things I have spoken to you, that you should not be made to stumble.
"They will put you out of the synagogues; yes, the time is coming that whoever kills you will think that he offers God service" (John 16:1-2).

2

Overwhelmed

I learned something in the psychiatric ward: doctors of psychiatry are not weird people, and the doctor assigned to me was a compassionate, understanding educator. She explained to me that the source of my panic attacks could be caused by chemical imbalances in my system, which could be caused by prolonged periods of stress. She further explained that part of my treatment would be devoted to helping bring balance back to my system. Above all, the most comforting thing I learned was I was not crazy. There was hope for me!

Each day, all the patients were required to participate in group sessions. After only a couple of sessions, I was encouraged by the fact that most of the other patients needed significant help, and I was not in that company. Looking back at my hospital stay, I now realize God was using that time to encourage me. Even on the brink of disaster, God was with me. However, I also realized there were demonic activities surrounding these mental disturbances. However, in my weakened state, it would take time for me to learn how to overcome these demonic attacks.

I had also undergone great loss, which I needed to process. From the time I gave my life to the Lord, I knew He had a plan for my life. When I felt the call to ministry, a brand-new sense of destiny and purpose filled my soul. I had discovered the reason for my creation! This sense of destiny kept me at my post and helped me endure all kinds of ministry hardships. When you know your life's assignment, you learn to **"endure all things" (see I Corinthians 9:12, 13:7; II Timothy 2:10).**

Behind the locked doors of the psychiatric ward, it felt like this "purpose" which had carried me since the day of my salvation eighteen years earlier simply evaporated. Never in my forty-three years had I experienced such loss and heartbreak. This heartbreak lingered long, which compounded my recovery. Concluding I had failed God made matters even worse. For those who have experienced such a loss, there is hope with many unplanned detours along the way.

Within a week of my admission, the staff felt confident enough to discharge me, and together my wife and I began our new journey into the unknown. Little did I know this next season would have important messages that would shape the rest of my life.

As the series of meetings concluded with the apostolic oversight team requiring my resignation, it was apparent there was no plan for us going forward or for our restoration. My wife was more direct: "You can't just leave us like this. You have brought us to the edge of a cliff and pushed us off. What are we to expect? What is your plan for us going forward?" We had been loyal followers of this movement for fifteen years and had supported our leaders through their own difficult moments, but my wife's questions were met with deafening silence.

As we arrived home after my hospital stay and faced the reality of our circumstances, it quickly became apparent we had many decisions to make. One redeeming factor was my separation pay would continue for six months. That was only God's mercy. However, throughout my years of pastoring, we had managed to set aside more than five times my severance package in church savings, so at least the church could afford it. Still, I was taking significant doses of medication, so I did not trust myself to make wise judgments about our future. So, the fallout continued, and there was much for us to process moving forward.

Shortly after my resignation, a letter from headquarters was sent to my former network of national and international leaders. The letter explained that I was no longer qualified as a minister of the gospel and announced the withdrawal of my ordination, which effectively closed the door for any continued association with that network.

When someone is drowning, we all hope a lifeguard will be on duty to save them. Charlotte, North Carolina, proved to be that place, and the lifeguards on duty there were Tommy Gable, Robin McMillan, and Rick Joyner. I later learned that each of these men had themselves been rescued, and each had the insight and compassion I needed and were currently pastoring.

After my resignation, Tommy Gable reached out to me and opened his church as a place for me to land in Charlotte.

Tommy had also once been shown the door out of our movement and understood what I was going through.

Tommy and Robin were both pastors in the Charlotte area, ministering in different churches, and had become friends over the years. Providentially, we rented a house across the street from Robin. Our kids were about the same age as theirs, so they quickly became friends. It was an ideal landing place for my family. While Robin was still in his own season of recovery, we often walked through the neighborhood together laughing, crying, and processing life and ministry, both good and bad. Today, I am not sure where I would be without those walks. Amid what seemed at the time a disappearing act by God, He remained ever present and faithful.

I was also amazed how through all this tumult, my children seemed cushioned from the blows, which can often have a lasting impact on the long-term survival of their faith. My wife and the Lord were the reasons for this outcome.

When we first moved to Charlotte in 1991, we had no idea Rick Joyner's ministry was located there. I had read some of Rick's early books and had been greatly influenced by his writings. The Sunday after our arrival in Charlotte, Robin invited me and my family to a cookout, and Rick and his family attended. When Robin introduced me to Rick, the first thing I said to him (which I'm now embarrassed to admit) was, "Well, Rick, I read your books, and they got me in big trouble!" While that was likely not the best thing I could have said, indeed Rick's writings rightfully challenged many church traditions and practices. Rick is a transformational leader, and his writings are a breath of fresh air.

Throughout my recovery, Rick provided timely, prophetic words which kept me afloat. He conducted weekly meetings every Friday and Sunday night, and the atmosphere in those meetings was electrifying and filled with the presence of God. Those who attended the meetings were filled with anticipation of what God might do. After the Friday night meetings, Rick often invited me to grab a bite to eat with him. These impromptu gatherings meant the world to me. I have long since maintained how important it is that we show up in people's lives at the right time. The attention Rick showed to me in those days was healing to my soul.

So, this was my rescue team, each designed with different skills, but all orchestrated by the unseen hand of the One who gives hope and restores.

During this time, I occasionally continued to struggle with panic attacks and anxiety. I can recall being invited to one pastors' gathering, and while driving back home, I became overwhelmed by great fear and anxiety. These feelings were overpowering, and I began to wonder if I could ever be free from such attacks. At the time, it was still a regular struggle for me to be around groups of people without feeling a dark cloud rising over me.

I was still endeavoring to learn my next steps. All we knew was Charlotte was where we were to spend the rest of our lives. Shortly after arriving in North Carolina, I began searching for a new profession. I felt that ministry was done with me, and I was done with ministry. After all, I needed to provide for three children and a wife, so I quickly began my job search. While we did have equity from the sale of our home in New Jersey, both my wife and I had purposed not to live off this. I think the Lord heard our pledge, so testing in that area continued.

As we began to settle in, I slowly thought about what I could learn from all that had happened. I was turning the page to a whole new chapter in my life, and there was much to be learned and unlearned.

After our arrival in Charlotte, it took me a while to grasp the purpose for this season in our lives. Ecclesiastes states, **"To everything there is a season, a time for every purpose under heaven" (Ecclesiastes 3:1).**

I am also keenly aware there is an army of people who have been wounded by the church. Like me, they have been sidelined, or may have concluded they were done with the church and the church was done with them. However, as horrible as this season might be, God weaves redemptive threads into the circumstances of our lives. Looking back, I will share some of the most valuable things I have discovered.

3

Silent Messengers

To place this in context, I need to give you some family background. I was raised in a strong, Irish Catholic family. I had a loving and respectful relationship with my mom and dad and three brothers. We were all accomplished athletes and had a good reputation in our community. Added to that respect, my oldest brother had determined to pursue the high calling of becoming a priest. After completing eighth grade, he went off to seminary studies.

However, prior to my brothers and me being born, a tragic event shaped our family. My mom had great difficulty with the birth of her first child, Kathleen. As a result of the damage that occurred during the birthing process, my sister was born mentally and emotionally disabled. Since my sister required 24/7 special care, by the time I was born five years later, Kathleen was institutionalized. While this brought further heartbreak to my parents, there was no other option for them at the time.

Such traumatic events can result in major, life-changing adjustments. Some respond with bitter resentment asking, "How could God allow such tragedy?" Yet my parents chose a different route: a life fully dedicated to God. This determined and intentional response led them to begin each day by attending Catholic Mass. Each day, as a family, we rose early in the morning, Mom and Dad ensured their four boys were properly dressed, and off to church we went. My early morning paper delivery route preceded our church attendance. This family practice of attending Mass continued daily from as far back as I can remember until seventeen years later, when I left for college.

This practice of putting God first was further reinforced each Christmas morning when our parents blindfolded us, so we could not see our presents before we went to church. I must admit, those early Christmas morning church visits did not make the most devoted and focused Hardiman boys, but they did make a lasting impression on us.

I had been in ministry for more than ten years when the Lord randomly began talking to me about my sister, Kathleen. He said, "Your sister was a silent messenger to your family! Without the ability to speak, her life became a message far more powerful than 10,000 preachers!" I immediately understood that God had used the most painful circumstance in my parents' life to make an important course correction from which they never deviated. In that moment, I saw my sister's soul imprisoned in her body, yet in eternity she would be credited for all the good fruit she had produced in and through our family.

All our lives we were told my sister had the intellect of a six-month-old. Nevertheless, we visited her at the institution on a regular basis. Kathleen never walked or talked, and when we were with her, she seemed to be in a world all to herself. Since she never made eye contact, we assumed she did not know we were there. This was reinforced by a staff member who told us Kathleen did not recognize anyone. However, years later, after a God-orchestrated event, my opinion of this would change dramatically.

Several years ago, while on a ministry trip to New Jersey, I was contacted by my older brother, who informed me that Kathleen was in the hospital and that the staff was concerned she might not survive. The church I was visiting was close to the hospital, so that afternoon I went and visited her. I prayed for her healing, and thankfully she made a quick recovery, but as usual she never recognized or acknowledged my presence.

Later that evening, I was at the church when the pastor informed me there was a couple there who had come specifically to meet me. I was surprised since my coming to the church had not been announced. I was also curious how this couple could know I would be at this church on this night. So, I asked, "How did you know to come to this church tonight, and why did you ask to see me?" They said the Lord had told them to come meet me.

The family had recently moved to the U.S. from South Africa and had four children, all with special needs. Some were mentally disabled; others had severe forms of autism. They wanted to meet with me because they knew I came from MorningStar. They said their children had begun to prophesy things like what Rick Joyner had written in his books and had a message for me.

I said, "That's interesting. Just this afternoon, for the first time in years, I saw my sister who is mentally disabled, and here you are on the same day for what seems to be a divinely arranged appointment."

I explained to them my sister's condition, then hastened to add, "She only has the intellect of a six-month-old." They said, "Don't believe it. The next time you see her, talk to her like you would speak to anyone else. Many such children live all day in the presence of God and are simply trapped inside their bodies!"

I just stood there in disbelief but could not deny how heaven had seemed to arrange this meeting. As I walked away, I had much to process. The next day, on our way home, I suggested to my wife that we stop by the hospital again to see my sister. Upon arrival, I asked the attendant if we could have a few moments alone with her.

My sister sat in her normal slumped over position and did not focus. However, I did not let that deter me from following through on the advice given to me by that South African couple. I said, "Kathleen, I am your brother Tommy. I want to tell you that, all our lives, we have been told that you don't know who we are, but if you can understand me, can you make some sign or gesture to let me know you understand what I am saying?" With that, my sister sat up like someone coming to attention, lifted her arm, and gave me a thumbs-up sign!

Then I asked her another question: "Would you like Jesus to live in your heart?" A tear rolled down her cheek. This was one of the most astonishing moments of my life.

On the day my sister passed away, I could only imagine the reunion she must have had with my dad and mom greeting her, as she passed from this life into her heavenly reward. I would have loved to have heard the first words spoken by my mother to her daughter, who was now made whole. My sister is now enjoying her eternal rewards.

Such tragic life circumstances are often silent messengers we must not miss. God used the pain of that tragedy to help my parents make a life-changing adjustment. My life circumstances were my silent messengers sent to speak something profound to me. This was my glimmer of hope during those dark days. God was looking for me, too, to make some major course adjustment. We must be keenly aware of these silent messengers God sends to communicate with us.

The word "illumination" means spiritual or intellectual enlightenment. Proverbs 1 gives us a picture of wisdom crying out in the streets waiting to be heard. It also gives us a picture of people who are counted among the simple ones who never seem to discern the meaning of their moment. In time, as I began to get my feet back under me, my cry was that I would discern the meaning of my silent messengers, and that is my prayer for you in this hour.

As I look back now on the leaders of that movement I connected with, I see an unwholesome view of kingdom relationships and the principles that govern those relationships. There is a godly and healthy place for commitment and loyalty, but taken to the extreme these principles can be used to bind people in ways God never intended. I had embraced those teachings so deeply I likely never would have left had I not been shown the door. Today, the silent messengers of my circumstances still speak clearly to me. God did not intend for me to be rejected. Instead, He wanted to release me from the prison of those misused, misapplied, and abusive beliefs.

In the end, the leaders of that movement embraced and taught many righteous things, and today I choose to believe they did not intend to hurt or misuse God's people, but they did. Though Martin Luther was a powerful, prophetic voice in his time and confronted many of the abuses in the church of Rome, he also taught and mistaught things about the Jews which became seeds that gave birth to the Holocaust. Today, while I still adhere to the principles of ministry, loyalty, and commitment to the cause for which God has joined us to others, I also realize all men have "feet of clay" (character flaws). My silent messenger has taught me our supreme devotion belongs only to One!

4

Teachable Moments

In 2014, my daughter, Kate, was pregnant with her second child. In the twenty-eighth week of her pregnancy, our grandchild was diagnosed with a tumor on her face, neck, and shoulder. The week before, we were praying fervently when the Lord spoke and told me my daughter's life was in jeopardy with this pregnancy. The ultrasound reinforced this word.

Over the next few weeks, as our family and friends stormed the throne of grace, we watched God remarkably intervene at every turn. One miracle after another took place, and eight years later we have a healthy, miraculous girl who is ready to take charge of her world. Sloane, whose name means "warrior," is known as "the miracle baby" in two hospitals. She is a testimony to answered prayer.

I call Sloane our "special gift" from God. As we stood in the gap for a miracle and fervently petitioned God, I sent a message to my children and close family members stating that, while I believe God is with us through it all, we must not miss what God is saying to us in this "teachable moment." Shortly after, my daughter wrote this as she reflected on their situation:

He makes beauty out of ashes. Have you ever sat around to think about what that actually means? I have, and I know firsthand out of our own pain and struggles, there is joy that might not have been found without walking THROUGH it.

I've contemplated this space, blog, or whatever you want to call it for a VERY long time. Back in January, one of my best friends told me I should start a blog and run a half marathon. She told me I needed to set goals for myself. I distinctly remember laughing and saying, "I hate running, and I have nothing to say." For some reason I'm now doing both. At points while typing I've asked myself why, but then realized, why not? It may be hard and scary, but you know what's worse? REGRET. So, here I am attempting to be vulnerable and real about raising a medically complex child and walking this unknown path, all while trying to manage being a good wife, present mom, daughter, sister, friend, employee, etc. Let me be honest; it's HARD and lonely at times.

Often, I wished there was a road map for our journey, wishing, hoping, and praying for answers. Four years ago, when our lives were turned upside down, I remember Googling some of Sloane's conditions. There wasn't much to read, and the doctors couldn't tell us anything definitive about her future. Instead, we live in six-month increments, with appointments and therapies in between MRIs, believing everything is stable.

What I've started to realize during these waiting periods is that maybe it's better this way. I don't want a diagnosis defining our future of what she can and cannot do. I want to push her forward to be the best she can be. I remember telling the doctors that she can do everything everyone else does, until she shows us differently. Guess what? So far, she does everything! We were told she wouldn't hear out of her right ear. Yet, when I whisper in the ear that is sutured shut and tell her she's a superhero, she repeats back to me what I've said. When the doctors told us she wouldn't be an athlete because of the tumor on her cerebellum, she started her first soccer season.

It's incredible to see a child overcome the supposed limits of a diagnosis. So, I said all that to say this: I hope this will be a space of hope and lots of laughter and learning together how to navigate the everyday challenges of raising medically complex children but doing it gracefully and with JOY.

In the book of Joshua, there are great and victorious moments but also setbacks. The valley of Achor proved to be such a place. Achan, a son from the tribe of Judah, took forbidden spoil from the city of Jericho, which resulted not only in his own death but also that of his family. All this happened in the valley of Achor, which means "valley of trouble." There are only three references in the Bible to the valley of Achor, which are all messages for those in low places. In Isaiah 65:10, God says Achor is a place of joy and prosperity **"for My people who have sought Me."** Hosea 2:15 says, in this same valley, there is **"a door of hope."** Some of the most troubling places in our lives can also become the most fruitful and prosperous. In times of trouble, there is always a "door of hope."

I was not viewing the season following my resignation objectively, not even close. I was simply too broken emotionally. However, every so often I would have glimpses of what I could learn from my situation and what God was speaking to me. This was the redemptive thread that revealed itself ever so slowly, while also appearing as my door of hope. Some thirty years later, I can look back and encourage you that, in all those terrible moments, God was teaching me things I never would have learned had I not navigated those troubled waters.

Depression is a cruel master. In this season, try as I might, this dark cloud seemed to follow me wherever I went. At times it was more gripping than others, and it would especially show itself at night. I must say there is a place to seek medical attention for certain conditions. However, I learned that the devil would attempt to piggyback himself onto my circumstances to fan my emotional struggles into full fury. What proved to be a major turning point was also a difficult midnight encounter.

I rose quietly out of bed, so as not to wake up my wife. I went to the downstairs sofa while wrestling with my emotions when my wife suddenly made her midnight appearance. Somehow she knew I was having a hard time. So, she sat next to me and began to pray over me in the Spirit. She did this for about ten minutes, and as she prayed I felt a lifting of the dark cloud that was haunting me. By the time she finished praying, I felt much better. After she went back upstairs to bed, I was significantly relieved but also a bit disturbed. I thought, why couldn't I do that? And how did my five-foot-two-inch wife become so powerful?

Here was my teachable moment: The next time I began to wrestle with this dark cloud, rather than give into it, I began praying in the Spirit (showing that I, too, could be as powerful as my wife). Sure enough, after about ten minutes of wrestling, that dark cloud began to lift off me! I discovered something important in that moment: Beside my circumstances or some chemical imbalance in my system, there was also demonic involvement behind my emotional problems.

Here is my conclusion today: These were second-class demons troubling me, and with some effort on my part, I could break their grip over me. While this may not sound like a profound revelation, for me this was a major teaching point and breakthrough. From that time on, in my valley of Achor, I discovered my "door of hope." I have shared this at various times while ministering, and it has brought breakthrough to many others as well.

Looking back through the years I can pinpoint another situation that unfolded with our oldest son, Brian. Though it was not a life-altering circumstance, it became a teachable moment for us.

From the time Brian was little, he loved sports but was particularly drawn to basketball. With my background in sports, I loved coaching my kids and did so until they were in high school. From a young age, Brian desired to excel in basketball. When he was nine, I coached his local basketball team, which was undefeated. We had only one more critical game remaining against the other top team, and Brian's hope for a victory in this championship game was high.

Even more importantly, this game was about capturing an opportunity. Teachable moments are often cloaked in desperation when we are hoping things will go our way. In moments like these, our spirits are open to learn important life lessons, yet all too often we fail to recognize those moments and squander the opportunities.

So, when my son and I talked about the upcoming game, I suggested we fast and ask the Lord to help us with this victory. Up to that point in his life, I can't remember him giving himself to a spiritual effort like he did this. He was earnest! As he described it:

I had been nervous about the upcoming championship game. As I fasted and prayed, I asked God for a confirmation and asked Him to show me the number 311. It was a random number I selected, but the number turned out to be much more than a confirmation for my championship game. What it did was make the Lord very real to me. I saw the number everywhere. I would wake up in the morning at 3:11 a.m., then I'd catch the clock again at 3:11 p.m. At one point I was watching an infomercial and the number "311" flashed across the screen as it listed 311 ways this product could be used. It was a huge comfort to me knowing God was with me as our team readied for the game.

We in fact won that championship, but more importantly I knew the Lord had heard my request. 311 became a way for me to always know the Lord was speaking to me, giving me confirmation, and knew what I was going through. It was a wonder to me in those years that the

Lord had me on His mind among the millions of other issues in the world.

When I applied to transfer from Drexel University to UNC Chapel Hill in my freshman year, I was accepted but continued to pray about my decision, making sure the Lord was in this move.

I entered UNC as a sophomore, and as I attended classes that first week, it became apparent that many students already knew each other. The search for new friends was difficult, but I met a student named Matt, who was also from New Jersey. We were in many of the same classes, and at the end of the day, I asked for his name on Instant Messenger so we could talk later. When I saw his Instant Messenger name, my jaw dropped. His nickname had the number 311 at the end.

I was overwhelmed. I thought, Lord, You have prepared this friendship for me. You paired me up with this individual to help in the transition from New Jersey to North Carolina, from Drexel to UNC Chapel Hill. This awareness that God was with me really shaped the rest of my college experiences.

The Lord showed me the number 311 to let me know He would be with me no matter what, and that He would never forsake me no matter what I was doing. Even if I was messing up, the Lord would be there looking out for me. He would be with me through all my circumstances, and God was letting me know He cared.

To this day, 311 has been a reminder that, whether I'm waiting for a job interview, or a phone call, 311 means, "Hey Brian, I hear you calling out to Me. I hear you and I love you. You're important to Me. Things may not always go your way, but I'm always going to be right here for you."

That was a powerful assurance for our son. These teachable moments set a pattern for how Brian would seek the Lord at various crossroads in his life. Some lessons are for a lifetime.

5

Waiting for the Perfect Correction

My son Michael played Division One college basketball and was not getting the play time we thought he should. However, on his first start against Davidson College, he finally had a chance to display his talent. In the first half of the game, he outplayed and outscored their star player, Steph Curry. However, the second half was another story.

In the next game, he returned to the bench even further down in the rotation. I then offered my son some advice: "Mike, you need to take good notes. I mean, really begin to journal things you are learning while sitting on the bench. There are things I learned while sitting on the Olympic team bench I could have never have otherwise learned."

Bob Jones, a well-known prophet who lived nearby, had given my son Mike a prophetic word while he was the star player on his high school team. He said that God was going to use his athletic talent to inspire and minister to others.

Mike's college coach ruled by fear, intimidation, and much cursing. It is not a style I think is successful. I told Mike, "Sometimes when an individual has a great calling on their life, God puts them under a bad leader. Consider the call on David's life under Saul. God arranged this season for David, so he would learn how *not* to be a king!" Mike took good notes and went on to serve as the athletic director and head basketball coach at our Christian school. He turned a floundering, winless basketball team into conference champions several times. Mike took good notes!

There was a man of God I greatly admired as a genuine apostolic father. The respect I had for this man continued to grow as I observed the love and esteem his spiritual sons had for him. This man was a true father in the Lord, and his network of four hundred pastors was impacting nations. In my time of distress, I reached out to him, and though I was not a part of his network, he graciously agreed to meet with me. In my one-hour breakfast meeting, he listened to my tale of woes. As the meeting closed, he reached over to me, grabbed my hand, and said these simple words: "Tom, it is going to be okay!" There was a fatherly weight to his words, and because of his years of experience, I believed him.

He was raised in a legalistic church. His father, a very stern man, was the senior pastor of that church. This man, whom I considered one of the great fathers of the faith, felt he could never please his dad. So, as a young man, he developed resentment toward his father. In a profound encounter at the age of nineteen, the Lord spoke to him saying, "I want you to go and thank your father for all he has taught you!" This man snapped back at the Lord, "Thank him? Thank him for what? With all my trying, I can never please him. What do you mean, 'thank him?'" The Lord responded, "You have had nineteen years of training on how *not* to be a father!"

Though his training was in an adverse environment, this man had a profound destiny to become a spiritual father to many! Sometimes the best lessons we learn are from the people God permits in our lives, who make powerful impressions of things we are not supposed to do. So, when he went to thank his father, his dad's response was predictable: "I've been waiting a long time for you to appreciate all that I've done for you!"

My son learned much about leadership playing college basketball, though the most lasting impressions that shaped his approach to coaching were negative.

In my most difficult season, it was now my turn to begin to draw upon all I had been through. While I was thankful for all I had learned in my first sixteen years in that system, I learned much about how *not* to pastor other leaders. God wanted these impressions to be etched deep in my soul, and they still shape how I lead today.

The method of correction and adjustment my former apostolic oversight brought to me was vengeful and cruel. I understand why soldiers returning from battle suffer post-traumatic stress disorder. My reaction to meetings which sometimes lasted more than twenty hours, and once for three days fielding questions predicated on false or partial information, was vicious and horrendous. It was shame-based and in no way reflected the heart of God.

Their decisions unfortunately destroyed a church of more than three hundred and unleashed a critical spirit that I believe, some thirty years later, still affects that region. For me, as I rehearsed in my mind everything that was said about me, I became a shell of my former self. Words are powerful and impactful. Later, as I began to recover, I recalled a saying I had heard some time ago, "Your enemies will tell you things your friends never will." While I do not believe this is the way to be a friend, there is truth in that statement. Our enemies can speak a measure of truth we need to hear.

In today's Western Church, preachers are only expected to tell their congregants what they want to hear, such as how Christian principles can benefit their lives. There is also a tendency to invalidate words that call for correction or adjustment because they did not come through a pure vessel. We can miss so much of what God wants for us when we listen through these filters. As I gathered myself up after those meetings, was there some gold in all that debris? Yes. Just because those meetings were so outrageous, were there any takeaways worth my attention? Again, yes.

Here is one such important lesson I have since incorporated into my leadership style: When it came time for Jacob and Esau to be reunited, Esau requested that Jacob hasten the pace of his return. Jacob's response to this speaks volumes of wisdom to those responsible for leading God's people. One of the criticisms aimed at me that was repeated more than once was the pace that I set for my congregation.

> **Then Esau said, "Let us take our journey; let us go, and I will go before you."**
> **But Jacob said to him, "My lord knows that the children are weak, and the flocks and herds which are nursing are with me. And if the men should drive them hard one day, all the flock will die.**

"Please let my lord go on ahead before his servant. I will lead on slowly at a pace which the livestock that go before me, and the children, are able to endure, until I come to my lord in Seir" (Genesis 33:12-14).

One does not become an Olympic athlete without some intense drive and determination. In fact, my entire athletic career was marked by intensity. In certain instances, this intensity can be refined into a godly trait, but it can also spill into your life and ministry in less-than-sanctified ways. While there were a host of other criticisms, my former apostolic team identified this as an area that needed adjustment. There certainly is a difference between leading and driving a flock. During my years on the sidelines, I have learned the important distinction between leading and driving, and today I think this is a strength in my ministry. Had I waited for this correction to come through a perfect vessel, I would have missed an important building block the Lord had for my future.

Many God-called leaders are Type A personalities. This personality type is often needed when attempting to birth something for God. However, the pace at which I led my congregation was not sensitive to the entire church's ability to keep pace. There were too many meetings, too many prayer gatherings, and too many church activities. Church leaders need to give attention to this message, lest we overburden God's people. I later understood that I was guilty of this infraction.

One final note on this topic: When God listed the indictments against the Old Testament leaders, it said: **"but with**

force and with cruelty have ye ruled them" (see **Ezekiel 34:4 KJV**). In certain instances, this indictment meant they led by the strength of their personalities. A charismatic personality can persuade a flock that theirs is a godly pace. However, over time, many of God's people will "burn out" in such an environment. It was my hope that, if God ever used me again, this sin would never again be laid at my door.

As leaders we must find the proper corporate pace for our congregations. In my experience, many church leaders do not know how to pace their churches, and some are driven by less than godly motives.

Over the years, I have learned to make adjustments to my life and ministry. As one blessed brother and friend, who knew me as a minister in my first pastoral assignment and on the other side of this great valley said, "We have known the old Tom and the new Tom. We prefer the new Tom!" Out of that mess, had I not gleaned from this valuable lesson, I would have missed an important stop along God's rocky road.

6

Resting

As we began the process of settling in Charlotte in 1991, there were still many unanswered questions. I had no clue what the heart of God was for our future. We only knew Charlotte was where we would spend the rest of our lives. So, I began job searching.

In the past, whenever at a crossroad, I would ask the Lord for direction. The word I kept hearing was "wait." Wait for what? This was my season of living in the dark.

We did, however, receive periodic prophetic words, visions, and dreams, all of which eventually made sense. Before we had even resigned from ministry, Mary Anne received a vision. In the vision, she saw a massive army of God's soldiers waiting for their general to inspect His troops. As the Lord worked His way toward us, He stopped periodically to give directions. However, when He stood in front of us, He instructed us to get out of the line. Then He informed us we were in no condition to fight. We were just too beat up and needed time to rest and recover from battle. In the vision, as my wife resisted, the Lord insisted! So, our resignation was our removal from the ministry. We simply needed time to rest and recover from this ordeal.

Rest is not something that comes easily to many people. It certainly did not come easily to the nation of Israel, which partly led to their Babylonian captivity. This was a forced sabbatical for the nation and for the land of Israel. Likewise, we were brought to a place of a forced sabbatical for our lives. Remember, the purpose of a sabbatical is to cease from your labors.

At times, government agencies require warning labels on products. Cigarettes have this warning on their packages: "WARNING: This product can be hazardous to your health." Ministry can also be hazardous. I have often mused that ministry should have a written warning label for those who dare enter. Jesus clearly warned His apostolic company about the hazards of ministry—at least twice:

> **And He said to her, "What do you wish?" She said to Him, "Grant that these two sons of mine may sit, one on Your right hand and the other on the left, in Your kingdom."**
>
> **But Jesus answered and said, "You do not know what you ask. Are you able to drink the cup that I am about to drink, and be baptized with the baptism that I am baptized with?" They said to Him, "We are able."**
>
> **So He said to them, "You will indeed drink My cup, and be baptized with the baptism that I am baptized with; but to sit on My right hand and on My left is not Mine to give, but it is for**

**those for whom it is prepared by My Father"
(Matthew 20:21-23).**

Jesus spoke of a cup of suffering and a baptism of fire.

**Then Jesus said to them, "All of you will be
made to stumble because of Me this night, for
it is written: 'I will strike the Shepherd, and the
sheep of the flock will be scattered.'
"But after I have been raised, I will go before
you to Galilee" (Matthew 26:31-32).**

The enemy is aware that if he can take out a leader, it will
have a multiplied effect on their followers.

So, here I was stricken, smitten of God, and the word
of the Lord to me was simply, "Wait and rest." I wish I had
been more compliant with that instruction, but I was still
struggling.

Rest, however, was not something I permitted myself to
enjoy. After all, I had to get on with finding a new profession for this season, though I had received this severe
rebuke from the Lord. Several months into my forced sabbatical, my job search had become fruitless, and my anxiety
increased as the equity from our home had dwindled.

About this time, I was invited to a pastors' gathering in
Raleigh. A very prophetic man, who had given me accurate
prophetic words in the past, walked over to me as I entered
the room and said, "That which God has intended as a
time of rest, you have made into a time of worry." Guilty
as charged!

Now, in overseeing MorningStar's network of ministry leaders, I have learned that most people consider rest optional. Even most congregants are unlikely to rest. There has been an erroneous concept taught that if we are not constantly producing and growing, we are doing something wrong. Yes, it is a godly mandate to bear fruit, but what tree bears fruit in every season? A healthy tree bears fruit *in* its season. In the Song of Solomon, when the king and future bride met, his first instruction was for her to rest. The king then instructed the others not to bother her until her time of rest was completed.

As a competitive athlete, I never enjoyed sitting on the bench, yet now this was my assignment. This prophetic word was right on, and I needed to yield.

7

Drydock

A few years ago, Mary Anne and I visited Boston Harbor. One of oldest ships, still in commission since the American Revolutionary War, is the USS Constitution. It was also in drydock. The Lord began to speak to me about ships, leader*ships*, and the purpose of drydock. All vessels must periodically undergo repairs to attend to what has happened below the waterline. Without such maintenance, the longevity of the vessel is jeopardized.

The history of the USS Constitution is interesting and speaks to us today. Its nickname is "Old Ironsides." It received this name because of the strength of the ship's hull. The vessel is constructed of Carolina Oak, which is an extremely dense wood. When the USS Constitution was attacked, cannonballs simply bounced off the sides of the vessel. This vessel was durable and at times seemingly indestructible.

It reminded me of people I have known in ministry—durable and at times seemingly indestructible. During my first fourteen years of ministry, my wife and I had been fired upon many times, yet we just kept on sailing. Many of our friends in ministry did the same. However, things were happening in the unseen parts, below the waterline, that would eventually need attention.

About twenty years after the USS Constitution's first commission, it became necessary for "Old Ironsides" to go into drydock. This visit for repairs revealed much about the overall condition of the vessel. Indeed, when the water was drained from around the vessel, it exposed a significant amount of barnacles which had attached themselves to its hull. These living creatures, called crustaceans, "glued" themselves to the ship and were living off whatever life they could extract from the wood of the ship's hull and became a drag on the vessel's sailing integrity. These stubborn creatures had to be scraped from the hull of the ship. If not, they will begin to grow a hair-like substance, and if drydock is delayed, this hair-like substance will begin to produce a beard-like growth. Sailors call this "Satan's beard." There is much in this prophetic picture to give heed to!

In its first drydock visit, ten wagonloads of barnacles were removed from the USS Constitution's hull. However, the second drydock would not occur until twenty years later. Because of this lack of maintenance, Old Ironsides' sailing integrity became slow and less maneuverable, earning her a new nickname, "The Old Slow Ship."

As we settled in Charlotte, we slowly began to realize this was a season God had set aside for our heavy, long-term maintenance. There were things that had happened below the "waterline" that needed repair, and there were some issues of structural integrity that needed to be examined. This season resulted in many barnacles being scraped from my hull!

Also, there were church people who had unfortunately attached themselves to us, who were not necessarily assisting with our overall mission. These individuals, year after year, can drain on the life of a church and its leaders. I had several relationships in my first years of ministry that drained life out of me. These same individuals also continuously sought counsel I had given them many times before. While I value all of God's people who are redeemed by His blood, during this season, God had to remove some of these relationships from my life. Drydock season is not to retire a ship but to restore its overall integrity and prepare it for its next commission.

On November 19, 2002, a vessel named "The Prestige" sank off the coast of Spain. The reason the ship sank was a condition called "hogging," which also affects the overall integrity of sailing vessels. Hogging is when the main support beam, or keel, of the ship bends upward. The keel is much like the sternum of the human ribcage. The sternum holds all the ribs together and is one of the main structural supports of the human body. If this upward arching or hogging becomes severe, the pressure can cause the keel to snap and sink the vessel.

People who are in prominent positions and who come under criticism can sometimes take a defensive posture like a cat called "getting your back up." If this condition is not given attention, it can sink your ship! In drydock, much attention is given to relieving this pressure caused by hogging.

When Moses struck the rock rather than speaking to the rock in the wilderness, this could very well have happened because of an accumulation of ministry frustration (see Numbers 20:10-12). Moses "had his back up"! This serious error resulted in Moses not entering the promised land. During this season in my life, the Lord also removed an accumulation of ministry frustration. Seasons of rest are for restoring vitality and fresh vision to God's people.

"Sagging" is another condition examined during drydock. In this condition, the main support, or keel, bends downward instead of upward. Throughout this ministry ordeal, I suffered significant depression. Our family doctor was so concerned he put me on antidepressants. The first prophetic words I had received from Bob Jones said that I had breathed in some bad air and that the Lord was in the process of helping me work this bad air out of my system. This "bad air" was not only the bad traditions and practices of our movement, but also word curses and witchcraft which had been pronounced over my life. My keel was sagging.

Weighty words coming from those in authority can have far-reaching, devasting effects on people. Even inflections or unkind words can take weeks or years from which to recover. Believe me, during my athletic career, I had my fair share of harsh coaches and corrections. However, harsh criticisms coming from spiritual leaders can create more lasting or permanent damage. Bob Jones later ministered to me and broke the "power of the spoken word," which had damaged my keel. During that time, I made it my goal, should God ever call me back to ministry, to speak words of life to those whom God had entrusted to me. God was fixing the sagging in my soul. He wanted my vessel to sail again, and during my drydock season, this was one of His main focuses.

People in ministry have silent killers. Year after year, people endure criticisms in ministry thinking they are "Old

Ironsides" and will just keep sailing. A visit to drydock may be more necessary than many think, and in my case, it saved not only my ministry but also preserved my marriage and children.

Inevitably, when I speak about drydock, the question is asked: "How can I do that?" "I can't afford to do that." Of course, the standard response is, "You can't afford *not* to." Still, every situation is different, but drydock should be happening more often. In our own situation, as our drydock season came to an end, we exhausted nearly all our cash. While there was a little reserve in our retirement account, being unemployed for nearly two years cost us a lot. It certainly was a financial sacrifice. However, what God did by rewiring our spiritual DNA paid great dividends toward our future. Spiritual leaders need this more than we realize. Even congregants who have been faithfully involved in the rigors of ministry can benefit from a season of drydock.

Every year at MorningStar, Rick Joyner insists that we close our church for the entire month of July. Yes, close the church—no meetings, no offerings, no leadership team meetings—nothing! While this may be a novel concept for most, let me explain the results. The Lord speaks to us much more during this time than at any other time of the year. Most of the significant words I have received personally over the last eighteen-plus years have come during our time of rest. Likewise, during the COVID lockdowns, we all spent several weeks in forced isolation. I trust we all spent that time wisely. During that time, away from the daily grind of ongoing ministry, my prophetic ministry became much sharper and more significant.

For some leaders, God wants to rewrite or add to your spiritual DNA. Your vessel needs to be refitted. He does not want to decommission or retire you, but like the USS Constitution, He wants to remove the barnacles that are draining the life out of you. Once refitted, the USS Constitution became sleek, more maneuverable, and battle-ready again. Today, the USS Constitution is not only the oldest commissioned ship in the U.S. Navy, but also the oldest commissioned ship in the world that is still afloat!

We all greatly value our relationship with the Lord and with church life. And with that, prophetic words of direction are precious to us. In the Song of Solomon, there is a description of the Shulamite woman stumbling upon a king. In this picture, she asks the king not to look at her because she has become unattractive from all the labor her "brothers" have required of her. As we read between the lines of this encounter, it seemed unreasonable labor was required of her. However, instead of judging her brothers for what was unreasonable, she judged herself as inferior.

The Song of Solomon was in part written to help us understand what it is like to have a one-on-one relationship with *our* King. This first chapter of the Song gives us a glimpse into the average life of a believer. The woman has been overworked and exhausted.

Sadly, this is an accurate picture of many people's church experience. The 20% of God's faithful saints who often carry 80% of the responsibilities are overworked and exhausted. All too often, we prop up programs and agendas God never authorized. Some of these precious people need time to rest and recover from the rigors of their labors and responsibilities.

However, such also need to keep in mind that, like the woman in the Song, when asked where they may be found, their answer should be, **"following in the footsteps of the flock" (see Song of Solomon 1:8)**. We should be found *with* and *in* His flock. Many of God's people need to come aside and rest *without* becoming alienated from their local assembly. I have watched many people over the years become bitter toward the local church and its leaders. Bitterness is a poison that will not only defile you, but can also defile many others, as Hebrews 12:15 warns.

Barna Research has stated that, over a ten-year period, "born again" believers who no longer attend church increased from 12.5 million to 18 million. This trend is very concerning. The clear biblical instruction is not to forsake the assembling of ourselves together (see Hebrews 10:24-25). During this time, Mary Anne and I had valid reasons to walk away from the formalized church. After all, the greatest pain we experienced and the deepest hurts and abuse we received came from church leaders.

I believe the reason most people walk away from church is because of offense, unmet expectations, or as Mike Bickle says, "God will often offend the mind to reveal what is in the heart." I tried my best not to let offense govern my responses to the disasters we experienced in church life.

However, this was a high mountain to climb. God helped us find grace in that season by connecting us with a new church family at MorningStar. While no church family or network is without defects, God reconnected us to His body, and MorningStar became our new tribe.

As I write this, many people are finding new life in local assemblies. God is again blowing afresh on our local assemblies, and this fresh breeze indicates that our spiritual winter is coming to an end.

8

The Hidden Hand

You may have heard this: "You don't want to know how sausage is made." While the finished product may be something to be desired, the production process is never pretty.

During my years of struggle, I searched for information to help me understand how God makes leaders. He is the author and the finisher of our faith. When Jesus called Peter, James, and John to follow Him, He said, **"Follow Me, and *I will make you* fishers of men" (see Matthew 4:19, italics added).** The question then becomes, "What did He do to make them what He called them to be?" The tense of that verse indicates an ongoing process. Jesus fashioned them into the leaders He wanted them to be.

After all I had been through, I wanted to understand how God worked in my life. While I felt I was a failure and inadequate to be used again, surprisingly, my failures indicated God still wanted to and could use me. As I researched biblical leaders, I better understood the process God uses to make us what He wants us to be, and it's not always pretty! This was extremely helpful in understanding what had happened in my own life.

As the saying goes, "You don't know what you don't know." What we don't know can cause significant destruction in the lives of God's people. Hosea 4:6 states, **"My people are destroyed for lack of knowledge."** Far too many seem unaware that the problems and struggles they are facing are often the Lord's hand making them into the person He has called them to be.

> **"My people are destroyed for lack of knowledge. Because you have rejected knowledge, I also will reject you from being priest for Me; because you have forgotten the law of your God, I also will forget your children" (Hosea 4:6).**

The word translated **"destroyed"** here is used in other prophetic books, like in Isaiah 6:5 and Jeremiah 14:17. Both speak of weeping or deep regret. Leaders who help people understand what is happening to them are truly gifts from the Lord (see Ephesians 4:8-11). The Lord has also promised to raise up pastors who will feed God's people with knowledge and understanding (see Jeremiah 3:15).

I believe we will see this great promise fulfilled more and more in the days to come. When I was told I was washed up and unfit for service, those words hung over me like a huge neon sign. Rejected, scorned, and despised by my peers and leaders, I didn't know if I could ever come back. Had God also rejected me? By the grace of God, I found leaders who helped me see what God was doing in my life.

Now fast-forward twenty years, and I have the privilege of teaching at MorningStar University. One of my responsibilities is to develop fresh course materials to inspire our students to a higher level of dedication. In my lecture notes, I introduced the topic "The Making of a Leader" as one of the most important truths I have ever presented. Since I came to grips with the process God uses to create leaders, this truth has become one of my most valued, foundational understandings of the Christian life.

During this time, two books impacted me, both with the title *The Making of a Leader*. One is by Frank Damazio, and the other is by Robert Clinton. Damazio was the pastor of City Bible Church in Portland, Oregon, then Vice President and Director of Ministers Fellowship International, a network of four hundred Christian leaders. Clinton was Professor of Theology at Fuller Theological Seminary in California.

From these writings, I drew some major truths that helped me during my season of struggle. Also, in my primary role of overseeing MorningStar's network of leaders, I watched as our leaders found themselves in similar seasons of trials, testing, and development. The lessons I learned through my testing and studies have greatly helped me impart wisdom to those whom I had been given oversight.

In his book, Clinton presents a study he made of every leader in the Bible. Then, to further support his thesis, he and his students studied every leader in church history. Clinton found some remarkable patterns present in the lives of these developing leaders. Three of these leaders were confronted with obvious challenges.

Joseph received a dream from the Lord concerning his future, but the route God directed him to take was incredibly contradictory to his ultimate calling. He was arrested and imprisoned, then ascended to the throne.

Moses, at age forty, felt he was ready to fulfill God's call, yet was premature in his timing. In his zeal, he committed murder and was forced to flee to the wilderness. Then, after forty years in the wilderness, God decided Moses was ready, and Moses felt it was premature.

David was anointed king over Israel but found himself running from a jealous king for the next thirteen years. He evaded more than three thousand assassins (see I Samuel 24:2). Clinton found patterns of wilderness-like experiences so frequent, he could not help but conclude these seasons of perplexing challenges were a part of how God fashions leaders.

Hope began to arise in my heart as I studied the preparatory paths upon which great leaders have found themselves. Rocky roads, contradictory circumstances, disillusionment, despair—God uses all these things to prepare great leaders for great purposes. I finally received the illumination I needed to discover God's plan for all I went through, so He alone could receive the glory. Wow! God's unseen hand was all the while preparing me for my ultimate destiny. All the pain and bewilderment began to vanish as I gleaned insight and understanding from these great leaders.

Clinton then breaks down these leaders' life experiences into two basic patterns. The first pattern is "training season," when necessary skills are gathered to perform one's calling. This is also called the natural skills gathering phase. This phase often begins before people are saved. For Moses, this training season was in the schools of Egypt. Moses would later hone these skills to write the first five books of the Bible and to understand Egyptians' ways when he was called to deliver God's people from Pharaoh.

Likewise, Rick Joyner has said God showed him that many people would come into church leadership through professional sports. Sports was their training ground. God uses their sports and teamwork training as seminaries to prepare them for His work. Over the years, I have noticed that leaders who understand team concepts of ministry have distinct advantages over those who do not. Those who do not grow in this often do not achieve their full potential. The pattern for New Testament ministry is teamwork.

The second pattern Clinton identifies is what he calls "the developmental hand of God." In this season, the unseen hand of God writes a custom-designed curriculum to produce the necessary character traits needed for each leader's calling. This season is just long and hard enough to bring about lasting change in one's life. The unseen hand of God was evident in all Bible leaders.

For Joseph, it was the rejection of his brothers, his season of slavery, and the false accusations that were made against him. All this served to produce in him a pure heart and character that lasted a lifetime. For Moses, it was the lessons he learned on the back side of the desert. For David, it was his thirteen years of running from Saul and observing Saul's disobedience. All these served to illustrate the unseen hand of God. The longer or more difficult the preparation, the greater the significance of the call.

Damazio noticed similar patterns of development. He described the seasons of God's dealings as:

- Distress – trouble, to hem in
- Affliction – of the soul, the furnace of affliction
- Purging – to refine, purify, clarify by heat
- Pressing – to squeeze, to push on, crush
- Fire – intense heat

Damazio identified a variety of tests people will encounter while Jesus makes them fishers of men:

1. The Offense Test (John 6:66-71) God will permit things in our lives we do not understand to test our faith and commitment to Him.
2. The Being Overwhelmed Test (Psalm 61:1-8)
3. The Misunderstanding Test (Acts 7:23-29)
4. The Time Test (Exodus 3:4-10)
5. The Servant's Test (Philippians 2:6-11)
6. The Obscurity Test (Judges 6:12)
7. The Wilderness Test (Acts 7:29)
8. The Discouragement Test (Joshua 7:7)
9. The Failure Test (Luke 22:54-62)
10. The Success Test (Deuteronomy 8:11-19)

Looking back over my season of testing, I could relate to every one of these seasons of development God had custom designed for me. Some tests were more arduous than others, but each had a purpose from heaven written on it, which was necessary to my development. However, one troubling conclusion author Clinton arrived at was that not everyone arrives at their destiny. In fact, this conclusion is supported in Scripture, **"For many are called, but few are chosen"**

(see Matthew 20:16). Clinton concluded that about 20% of those called to their destiny make it to "their day of convergence."

Nearly everyone on the path to their destiny will experience a season of disorientation. One of the strongest indications that you are close to reaching your "day of convergence" is the desire to give up on your call. Consider how Joseph, Moses, and David felt in their seasons of deep testing. Those who rise to meet their day of destiny respond rightly when facing their burning bush.

By the way, there is much more at stake in your burning bush experience than you realize. The burning bush was not just about Moses and his call; it was also God's answer to the generations of people who brought their prayers before Him with deep cries for deliverance.

Now, when I look back at the second time God called me to ministry, I can see the faithful prayers of my mother, grandmother, and many others. People are praying desperate prayers right now, and their pleas are for God to help them! As stated, there is much more at stake than your future. Your positive response to God's call, a second time, could be God's answer to countless other prayers.

Of the ten tests listed in Damazio's book for those called to leadership, the test of offense is perhaps the most challenging. Everyone will eventually face this test.

In John 6, Jesus purposely put before His followers a saying that they would not understand: **"Unless you eat the flesh of the Son of Man and drink His blood, you**

have no life in you" (see John 6:53). That single statement resulted in many of His disciples no longer following Him. Offense in this case had to do with the expectations of His followers. Jesus had just fed the multitudes, so their expectations were for Him to continue providing daily bread. Once these superficial expectations were no longer met, they were no longer willing to follow Him.

In the mid-1980s, I heard a truth expounded by Bob Mumford, a great Bible teacher at that time. His topic was "offense." Bob unpacked the meaning of the Greek word *skandalon*, often translated "offense" in the Bible. He likened it to a trap and artfully explained how bait was prepared to lure unsuspecting prey into its clutches. Once caught, it was most difficult to extract oneself from this iron-like grip. His exhortation was not to get caught in this trap of being offended.

Years later, I had to walk this out. I did not want to be offended by those who had caused me to leave the ministry or had brought great trauma to my family's life. I did not want to abandon my call or my walk. Too much was at stake. Any decision I made through offense would have rippling effects on my wife and children. I could not afford to get off course. Then, just when I thought I had climbed this mountain, there was another mountain in sight which needed to be conquered.

Lest we think this is a problem that only happens to casual followers, think again. After John the Baptist was imprisoned, he seemed to have doubts about the man he once introduced as "the Lamb of God." John later instructed his disciples to ask Jesus, **"Are You the Coming One, or do we look for another?" (see Matthew 11:3)**. To reassure

John that Jesus was indeed the Messiah, Jesus instructed John's disciples to go back and tell John the authentic signs they were seeing and hearing. But then Jesus also issued a warning, saying, **"Blessed is he who is not offended because of Me" (see Matthew 11:6)**. John's expectations were different than what was unfolding, and Jesus did not want John to be drawn into that trap.

The warning that Jesus issued and that Bob Mumford so powerfully reinforced rings true today. Sadly, I have observed in my many years of ministry that offense is a big reason many people take detours and sometimes exit consistent church involvement. The expectations people had in John 6 were not much different from today. The reason church attendance has significantly declined over the past decade and half, in my humble pastoral assessment, is that people get offended and disappointed over unmet expectations.

Even in our halls of Congress, laws are being written and passed today to ensure that people and people groups are not offended. Sadly, this mentality has crept into the church. While the church must never become a place that intentionally causes offense, we must also realize that God Himself will offend our minds to reveal what is in our hearts.

Periodically, I must assess my own life to ensure that offense has not crept back in. Even after I thought I was on the road to recovery, something would invariably set off a chain of events which would show me there are still things in my heart that do not belong there. Bob Jones, a prophet, and a great friend, often told us, "You need to flush at the end of each day." In other words, get rid of anything that causes offense and get right with God each day. What great advice!

The book of Jonah is the only prophetic book in the Bible that is more about the prophet than the prophecy. Today, as the prophetic ministry gains more prominence, the clear message of Jonah must not be ignored. Jonah was offended by his prophetic assignment, resisted his assignment, then reacted in anger when Assyria repented.

Imagine God giving you a prophetic word that can change a nation in a day! Then you give that prophetic word, and the entire nation sees the error of their ways and repents. Then you react in anger to God's mercy on that nation!

To give some background to Jonah's reaction, we must understand the barbaric conflict between Israel and Assyria. The Assyrians were once comparable to modern-day terrorists. They plundered and ravaged the Northern Kingdom of Israel. Jonah's prophetic word called for Assyria's national repentance to forsake their evil and violent ways (see Jonah 3:8). Indeed, they did repent, but because of their history of terrorism toward the Jews, Jonah wanted to see God's judgment on them, not His mercy. So, Jonah was offended by God's mercy.

To illustrate how offense affected Jonah, offense sent him in the wrong direction. The Hebrew word used four times to describe that direction meant "down." Furthermore, Jonah had to pay the cost for that trip which took him in the wrong direction.

When we get offended, it can not only cause us to go in the wrong direction, but it can also be costly. However, there is more to extract from Jonah's offense. Jonah's misstep was not only costly to Jonah but also to all those around him. Everyone onboard that ship was led into a great storm because of Jonah's offense. When we become offended, we can pull those who are close to us into our storms. In my season of "great woe," the last thing I wanted was for my wife and children to be adversely affected by my harbored offense.

Another thing we can learn from Jonah's story is obedience to God. In the book of Jonah, the storm obeyed God, the east wind obeyed God, Israel's enemies obeyed God, the fish obeyed God, and even the plant obeyed God. The only one who did *not* obey God was Jonah, the prophetic man who carried an offense.

If being offended is like being trapped, what guidance can we find to avoid being offended? When we look in the Bible and at our experiences, most offenses can be traced to unfulfilled, unrooted expectations. In John 6, when many of Jesus' followers turned back from following Him, it was because of false hopes of an easier life. Jesus tempered those expectations by declaring to His followers, **"Whoever does not bear his cross and come after Me cannot be My disciple" (see Luke 14:27).** Factoring that statement into our journey with the Lord will certainly temper our expectations.

Another common trap of offense I have found is unrealistic hope and expectations of church leaders. True, there are certain standards by which church leaders should live, but those standards are not always kept.

The Song of Solomon uncovers many phases of the bride's development. In this marvelous study, the woman was asked to go to the mountain of myrrh, which represented her place of suffering. While reluctant, she accepted her king's request to go, and in chapter 5 she indeed suffered:

> **I opened for my beloved, but my beloved had turned away and was gone. My heart leaped up when he spoke. I sought him, but I could not find him; I called him, but he gave me no answer.**
>
> **The watchmen who went about the city found me. They struck me, they wounded me; the keepers of the walls took my veil away from me.**
>
> **I charge you, O daughters of Jerusalem, if you find my beloved, that you tell him I am lovesick! (Song of Solomon 5:6-8).**

The watchmen who were responsible for the safety of the city wounded and unveiled the woman. Fortunately for her, this only drove her deeper into her relationship with her king. Unfortunately, disillusionment and disappointment with a leader's conduct can be devastating to God's people, and not everyone recovers.

God does permit us to disagree with our leaders from time to time. And occasionally, we are exposed to their weaknesses and sinful conduct. David was constantly fleeing from the man who was the anointed king of Israel. Samuel was raised in Eli's house, the high priest whose corrupt and sinful sons fornicated in the tabernacle and took offerings designated to the Lord.

When events took a turn for the worst in my life, the heroes and church leaders of my early Christian walk became my greatest foes. As I began to understand the truth of how God develops leaders, I learned I was not alone. My experience was only part of the process God uses to develop leaders. My challenge was then to use that disappointment to drive me to know my King more deeply. My goal was to come out of the wilderness leaning on my Beloved.

There are also unrealistic expectations projected upon today's leaders. The average church member expects their leaders to be proficient in at least sixteen skills: preaching, teaching, worship leading, counseling, modeling a perfect family, and the list goes on. Unfortunately, the average leader can only be proficient in about four skills, so there is a great gulf between a leader's skills and expectations. These unrealistic expectations are a prime reason so many church leaders leave ministry today. Church leaders who learn not to yield to these expectations are part of the 20% who make it to their day of destiny.

Joseph is a great example of discerning the hand of God during his greatest moment of adversity. In Genesis 50, Joseph's father, Jacob, died, and his brothers were afraid Joseph might retaliate for the evil they did to him. Joseph gave an extraordinary response: **"As for you, you meant evil against me, but God meant it for good in order to bring about this present outcome, that many people would be kept alive [as they are this day]" (Genesis 50:20 AMP).** In that moment, Joseph showed his brothers forgiveness, not only because he saw the purpose of God for his life, but also to become the vessel God would use to preserve multitudes, including his family.

This reminds me of the story of the young boy who was assigned to clean the horses' barn. The young boy loved horses so much, at the end of the day when he was asked about his first day on the job, he remarked, "Well sir, you know, as I was cleaning all the waste, I kept getting more and more excited thinking there was every indication that horses must be in there!" That is called looking for good in every stinking situation! **"Good sense makes a man restrain his anger, and it is his glory to overlook a transgression or an offense" (Proverbs 19:11 AMP).**

I remember reading an article which said, "The church is the only institution that shoots its own wounded." I'm not sure that is entirely true, but it certainly was the case with me. We all have regular opportunities to overlook offenses. This Proverb indicates that overlooking someone's transgression or offense is a credit to our account.

On the cross, Jesus asked His Father to forgive those who crucified Him. Forgiveness not only diffuses situations but also brings healing to ourselves. Forgiveness and avoiding further offense were key to overcoming what was done to me. Meanwhile, several leaders who withdrew the right hand of fellowship from me and called me unfit for ministry are no longer in ministry. Some have retired, others have closed their churches, and still others have gone back to secular work. It is entirely by God's grace that I am where I am today.

The practice of praying for those who have wronged us is very freeing. Over the years, I have experienced great release from offenses that resided in my soul whenever I prayed for those who wounded me. If the church would practice praying for its enemies more often, many strongholds over God's people and churches could be broken.

"You have heard that it was said, 'You shall love your neighbor and hate your enemy.'

"But I say to you, love your enemies, bless those who curse you, do good to those who hate you, and pray for those who spitefully use you and persecute you,

"that you may be sons of your Father in heaven; for He makes His sun rise on the evil and on the good, and sends rain on the just and on the unjust.

"For if you love those who love you, what reward have you? Do not even the tax collectors do the same?

"And if you greet your brethren only, what do you do more than others? Do not even the tax collectors do so?

"Therefore, you shall be perfect, just as your Father in heaven is perfect" (Matthew 5:43-48).

9

There is Hope

The speaker at MorningStar's first conference was Mahesh Chavda. The first words of his message were about restoring all we have lost! He had my attention from the start. Further reinforcing his topic was a word repeatedly whispered in my spirit a few weeks prior. Could this be true? Was the Lord telling me He would restore my losses? To paraphrase Psalm 126, when Cyrus announced that Israel could return to their land, many of the Israelites thought that announcement was too good to be true. I had the same initial reaction. This *was* too good to be true.

Throughout the rest of the conference, the concept of restoration was repeated. At one point, Bobby Conner approached me and said, "The Lord is about to bring about some significant changes in your life." A change of seasons was being announced, and I was more than ready for this season of loss to be over.

Over the next few weeks, what became evident was the unseen hand of God guiding me and my family back to the land that had so mistreated us! At first, the direction to return to New Jersey was not a welcomed idea. However, to restore what had been lost required restoration in the presence of my enemies (see Psalm 23:5). Of course, there were fears of returning. Nevertheless, it became unmistakable that this was the guiding hand of God. During this time, there were several distinct confirmations to Bobby Conner's prophecy.

After this first conference, MorningStar's influence increased, and I received an offer to join the MorningStar staff working in a basic role. However, the day before I was to begin work, I received a phone call from the director of operations. He said, "The Lord spoke to me this morning that you are not the man for this job, but He told me to tell you to unpack your winter clothes because you are going back to New Jersey!" This was reinforced in a Friday night School of the Spirit meeting when a man I had never met, Graham Pitt, approached me and said, "I see you as a lighthouse, a life preserver, and a lifeboat, and God is going to send you to a place to rescue people."

Though I had not kept up with the condition of my former church in New Jersey, it was not doing well. It was not a huge leap to realize that people needed to be rescued. While the leaders of that movement had wrested the oversight of that church from me, they were not the real shepherds of that flock. I was told the church had dwindled from more than three hundred to about thirty, with many more bobbing in the water. To be perfectly honest, I did not want to go back to that hostile environment. Mary Anne also had strong opinions and concerns about going back.

Still, now that MorningStar had withdrawn its offer, and with little cash on hand and rent due, what were we to do?

You may also know God as "a last-minute God," or better yet, "a God who is right on time!"

The phone rang again. This time it was my brother-in-law, Mike Mulcahy. He said, "Tom, I need help with my Dad's construction company. I need someone in the office I can trust. I'd like to offer you a job to come back here." Was this the Lord? Mike asked, "So, Tom, what do you think?" I didn't have to think. I knew it was God. I said, "Yes, I'll take the job." Right on time, Lord!

The prospect of restoration, while exciting, is also not without its challenges. Yes, I needed to leave for New Jersey right away, but there were complications. Having a wife and kids and suddenly needing to move to New Jersey with no place to live simply did not work. So, we decided I would move back and live with my mother who needed help, while Mary Anne and the kids remained in North Carolina to finish out the school year. Then the rest of the family would move back. This forced separation proved difficult for many reasons. Still, we took comfort in the fact that restoration was underway.

There are aspects of restoration you will need to fight for and sacrifices you will need to make. When Cyrus issued the decree releasing the Israelites to return to their homeland, few chose to make that arduous 1,600-mile trip home. Most were settled in their new life and ways. However, God had raised up Cyrus to rebuild their temple, reestablish Jerusalem, and restore the purposes of God. Those who answered that call would forever have their names listed in the eternal records of Scripture.

We now faced the prospect of resettling in the place where we experienced rejection and pain. This was indeed a daunting task, but our season of loss was over, and God was about to show Himself strong on our behalf.

The Bible has much to say about restoration, but until I returned to the place I needed to be for that to happen, I did not fully realize the meaning of this biblical truth. At the time, I recalled Bob Jones' word that I had breathed in some bad air, but in time, God would work that bad air out of my system. Restoration is a massive biblical topic. The first three chapters deal with how man lost what God had intended for him in the garden. The last three chapters deal with how God restored all that man had lost in the garden. The rest of the Bible in between deals with God restoring everything man had lost.

I began to study biblical restoration, and here are some facts I found:

- People in need of restoration have seen better days.
- In most cases, pain and sorrow accompany those losses.
- Those losses come in a variety of ways:
  o accidental
  o neglect
  o poor choices (the Prodigal Son)
  o ill intent (thou shall not steal)
  o unwise decisions (Joseph sharing his dream with his brothers)

It became clear that no matter how the losses happened, I still qualified for God to restore them.

If we examine biblical restoration even more closely, the topic of loss is addressed again and again:

> In Exodus 21:33-36, if a man dug a pit and neglected to cover that pit, and another man's ox fell into that pit and died, that was an accidental loss. Though there was no ill intent involved, the man who dug the pit was required to restore the ox.

> In Exodus 22:1-2, when loss occurred through theft or ill intent, the required restoration was five oxen for the theft of one ox.

> In Proverbs 6:30-31, when loss occurred through premeditation by the perpetrator, the restoration requirement was even more severe—a sevenfold restoration was required, which signified a complete restoration.

> Even in Matthew 5:38, **"an eye for an eye, and a tooth for a tooth"** was built on the concept of fair compensation.

In God's restoration package, pain, suffering, and intent are factored into Old Testament law. Our Judeo-Christian court systems were built on this foundation and factored in pain and suffering as part of fair compensation for restoration.

As I began to seriously reflect on the last seven years of my life and all the losses I had suffered, coupled with this change of season, I began to develop hope that God indeed wanted to restore what I had lost.

It has been my practice not to judge the true heart motives of the people who came against us. However, after evaluating the actions of the leaders who came against me and the judgments they made, it sure felt like there was ill intent. A few years later, when I attempted to reopen lines of communication with the senior leader of that movement, his words were telling. One of the first statements he made to me in that meeting, knowing all that had happened—my hospitalization, loss of home, ministry, and way of life—was, "You got what you deserved!" Then, the actions they continued to take after my return to New Jersey further reinforced my conclusions. Still, their ill motives only further increased what God required to be restored.

Many people in God's kingdom have been mistreated, maligned, and misunderstood. Many have gone through difficult church disputes, conflict with poor leaders, divorces, and on and on. Sadly, many reputations have been destroyed with ill intent involved. For those who have walked down this dark road, my appeal to you is to hold on to the God who restores!

There are also many promises of restoration in the book of Joel. It was written during a time when Israel had forsaken the Lord and was worshiping the demonic fertility god, Baal. Often, this worship called for the sacrifice of children on white, hot altars to please this false god. For this idolatrous worship, the nation brought judgment on itself. However, despite reaping the fruit of their misguided ways, a gracious God charted a path forward for restoring their losses.

Joel 2 begins by calling God's people to repentance. The promise given is, if they turn from these evil practices, God will restore their losses. The following portion of Scripture contains some of the greatest promises in all the Bible. If those who suffered years of losses return to God, He promises to restore those losses. Such promises brought great hope to my spirit as well. Let's unpack them:

> **Be glad then, you children of Zion, and
> rejoice in the Lord your God; for He has given
> you the former rain faithfully, and He will cause
> the rain to come down for you—the former rain,
> and the latter rain in the first month.
> The threshing floors shall be full of wheat, and
> the vats shall overflow with new wine and oil.
> "So I will restore to you the years that the
> swarming locust has eaten, the crawling locust,
> the consuming locust, and the chewing locust,
> My great army which I sent among you.
> "You shall eat in plenty and be satisfied, and
> praise the name of the Lord your God, Who has
> dealt wondrously with you; and My people shall
> never be put to shame" (Joel 2:23-26).**

God has the unique capacity to restore lost years. As I reflected on the years and time spent recoiling from the events of my life, I felt there was no way forward for me. The vision I once had had vanished. Now I was simply trying to survive. These were my lost years. Surely Joseph, Moses, and David felt the same during their years of opposition, but God's promise was to restore those lost years. **With the Lord one day is as a thousand years, and a thousand years as one day" (see II Peter 3:8).** God can do in a day what would take man a thousand years. If God can give us the capacity to **"redeem the time" (see Ephesians 5:16;**

Colossians 4:5), He can give us the capacity to redeem lost time.

God also keeps a record of all that was lost during those lost years. Job was given twice as much as he lost. Somehow heaven kept track of that. Joel notes successive years of loss. Not only does God promise a new harvest, but also the restoration of losses suffered from lost years. To say it plainly, once God has determined to restore your losses, you not only receive a new harvest, but He also restores the harvest you missed years ago. What a God!

Amazingly, there is more. To understand this season of restoration more fully, we need to understand the heart of the Judge who orders these things to be restored. The heart of the Judge is evident in this passage: **"Then the Lord will be zealous for His land, and pity His people" (Joel 2:18)**.

The *Jamieson-Fausset-Brown Bible Commentary* further explains the heart of the judge. It portrays God as a righteous Judge who is a jealous husband, and who sees His wife has been dishonored. He then rises with flushed face and righteous indignation to correct the wrongs which were done to her.

God draws a line in the sand stating, "enough loss," and then seasons of loss come to an end. God then pledges to act on behalf of His beloved to ensure that the honor that is due them is restored.

As we returned to New Jersey, some amazing things happened. By the grace of God, our marriage and family were still intact, but it seemed nearly everything else was lost.

Our church, our house, all our years of ministry labor, and nearly all our finances were gone. My confidence was shattered, and our reputation was in the toilet, yet we had a promise of restoration.

During our time in North Carolina, members of our previous church had largely scattered. The promises of a new pastoral team and much better things when I was no longer their pastor never materialized. In fact, those promises were hollow. A church of more than three hundred had dwindled to a handful, and most who had scattered had never found a new church home. However, many had had time to adjust their harsh attitudes toward me.

Similarly, the Sunday after Joe Biden became president, I was assigned to speak at MorningStar. I had voted for the other guy. The Lord showed me an unrighteous wresting for control and power had resulted in Joe Biden becoming our president. I was shown these individuals would be in power for a while, but they would make a mess of things. As of this writing, a little more than two-and-a-half years into Joe Biden's presidency, the U.S. is in a mess. The Lord showed me that in similar fashion the control and power of my church had been wrested from me, but the mess that had been made after had turned the peoples' hearts back to me. Sure, I had made my own missteps, but God's hand was still on my life to lead His people through that season.

One unexpected thing that happened after our return to New Jersey involved the restoration of our finances. As stated, we suffered significant financial setbacks. However, without disclosing this to anyone, on more than one occasion, we were given checks for $10,000. And though we had sold the home we loved in New Jersey to move to North Carolina, somehow when we returned, we could afford a home that was even better than our previous residence.

As God directed us back to this land in this new season, things gradually began to unfold. Our old church continued to struggle, and the pastor who rose in my place closed the church, sold the building, and left town with half a million dollars to allegedly start another church in another state. It never happened. His decision to leave town with all the money only added fuel to the people's hurt and disillusionment.

Over the next few years, our financial situation continued to improve, but far more importantly, many fractured relationships were mended. Some people were misled and told things about us that were simply not true. Others who were outright hostile toward us stepped across the threshold of our rented church building begging for our forgiveness, which we were always quick to offer. Still other relationships never healed and continued to be adversarial, but God still vindicated us.

Such reconciliations were aided by our new perspective on ministry which I had gained while "sitting on the bench" in Charlotte. Armed with this newfound perspective, I could see how the "old Tom" and "new Tom" were different. Many liked the "new Tom" better and said so. Our season in Charlotte had rewired us. The "bad air" was out of my system. Though strong foundations and fundamentals of faith were taught and learned in our former movement, some of their traditions, systems, and practices were simply not of God. Additionally, the passion and drive acquired from my athletic training latched on to my zeal and approach to ministry.

When I stand before the Lord to give an account for my first thirteen years of ministry, I know there will be corrections. At times, these flaws and misguided practices hurt people, but I still did them thinking they were right and from the integrity of my heart. What helped reconcile these relationships was my honesty to admit my errors, make adjustments, ask forgiveness, and move on.

"He also chose David His servant, and took him from the sheepfolds;
"from following the ewes that had young He brought him, to shepherd Jacob His people, And Israel His inheritance.
"So he shepherded them according to the integrity of his heart, and guided them by the skillfulness of his hands" (Psalm 78:70-72).

As my season in the wilderness and opposition came to an end, I noticed something else had changed—me. All the hardships, heartache, and pain had negatively impacted me, but when I approached ministry the second time, I had something I did not have before. When people shared their stories of testing and suffering, my response was different. Instead of a manufactured response, I now had empathy toward others. God had added this to my life. I loved it, and the people loved it! God had not only restored me but had also given me something new that I would need for my next ministry assignment—compassion.

10

The Call to MorningStar

The phone rang again. It was the same man who had told me ten years earlier, "You are not the man for this job, but unpack your winter clothes because you're moving back to New Jersey!" This phone call was different. He said, "We just finished a conference, and something happened that involved you." I was puzzled since Mary Anne and I were not even at that conference.

He told me a speaker named Kingsley Fletcher, whom I had never met, had a word for Rick Joyner during the conference. In the middle of Kingsley's message, he walked over to Rick, covered the microphone, and asked him, "Who is Tom Hardiman, and who is Mary?" Rick said, "They're part of our MorningStar Fellowship of Churches in New Jersey." Kingsley said, "Well, wherever they are, they don't belong there anymore. They're supposed to be here working for you!"

He then shared another word that was given the following day by John Paul Jackson. Neither John Paul nor Kingsley knew about each other's words. John Paul's word was, "Is there a Tom H. here?" There were a thousand people at this conference, so one man named Tom H. stood up, but John Paul said the word was not for him. He delivered the word anyway. He said, "Tom H.'s ultimate destiny and calling is not where he now is. His destiny is here." These words rang true in our spirits and confirmed what God had been telling us.

He continued, "Rick would like to ask you to join his staff and oversee our network of pastors and leaders." This network is called MorningStar Fellowship of Ministries (MFM). At the time, the network had about a hundred leaders spread all over the globe. It was a high honor.

Over the years, I have reflected on my years of brokenness and heartache and remembered the names Joseph gave to his sons after all the injustice and mistreatment he endured. He named his sons Ephraim and Manasseh. Ephraim means, "He has caused me to be fruitful in the land of my affliction." Manasseh means, "He has caused me to forget." God is indeed a restorer!

What followed that phone call from MorningStar was a series of prophetic encounters and words which indicated our season of restoration and ministry in New Jersey was coming to an end. It had now been ten years since our return, and the church had grown to embrace its call to prophetic, "gap-standing" intercession for the state.

Additionally, we had conducted several successful prophetic roundtables in the Northeast. The hurt and disillusionment of the past had long been over, and God had restored our reputation with the people and ministers in the area. Over those ten years, we often had joint meetings with other churches and developed a close bond with African American Pastor Jerome Wilcox and his church in Trenton. Occasionally, we even hosted conferences which were encouraging to the church at large. Yet, amid these advances, something was shifting inside me.

In time, my heart became enlarged from caring for the flock to caring for pastors. My attention was broadening. Guest speakers who came to the church told me privately they saw my assignment changing from the local church to the church at large and returning to MorningStar. This happened on several occasions. Mary Anne and I were not surprised by these prophetic words because we felt the withdrawal of our roots in New Jersey on the horizon. In fact, for many months we had been praying the prayer of Jabez for God to enlarge our territory (see I Chronicles 4:10).

Mary Anne had also had several prophetic dreams which proved to be God's direction for us. Even before Kingsley Fletcher's word, Mary Anne dreamed we were in a pickup truck in a quarry behind Ray Hughes, a senior leader at MorningStar. In the dream, both of our trucks were loaded with construction material, but curiously, ours had an iron and an ironing board. Only when he pulled out of the quarry could we also go. We interpreted this to mean that when Ray left MorningStar, we would arrive. The day it was announced at MorningStar that Ray was leaving was the day it was announced we were coming.

Mary Anne and I anticipated this change happening sooner. We expected to move to MorningStar a year earlier than we did, but God had not finished His preparation process both for MorningStar and for our local assembly.

The couple we thought would pastor the church in our absence was not quite ready, so things were not yet in place. I remember a clear word I received from the Lord during this time. I was walking up the steps of the church when I heard, "You are not finished here yet. I want you to finish well."

When I was in the military, "short timers" was the term given to those who were about to be discharged from active duty. This statement was also often used to explain the cavalier or neglectful state these individuals were in just prior to their discharge. When Jesus was on the cross, the last statement He uttered was, "It is finished." We would all do well to complete the assignments the Lord gives us. So, we had determined to complete this phase of our assignment well.

For us, God "making all things beautiful in His time" was another year of pastoring the local assembly. And given the word to finish well, we purposed to give our best to the people of our church. God was making all things ready for this major shift—for us, the local church, and for MorningStar.

Another key dream Mary Anne had during this time was we were purchasing a new home. When the realtor showed us the property, our eyes were drawn to the property lines. Mary Anne asked if our property ended with the trees at the bottom of the hill. The realtor said, "Oh no, do you see those hills in the distance? *That* is your property line!"

God was being faithful to alert us that the winds of change were upon us. Other early prophetic clues included several dreams that we were on staff at MorningStar. Of course, at the time, we couldn't just call and ask the leadership to hire us. So, we just prayed, left it to the Lord, and waited for His timing.

Yet, these dreams and prophetic words were unmistakably God. Now, with wisdom, we needed to find a way to gracefully hand off our congregation to one of our local leaders. After all that our people had been through, the last thing we wanted was to damage the confidence restored in their hearts toward church leadership.

Yet, in these seasons of transition, God had all His bases covered. Danny McKeon, an elder in our church, and a man whom I had worked with for more than twenty years, was the man for the job. He had also remained faithful through those difficult years. He was a Joshua to me.

His wife, Chris, had been saved in our church and grew to be a powerful, prophetic voice. As of this writing, Danny and Chris still pastor the church. But now it was time for them to assume a more direct leadership role, and it was time for Mary Anne and me to start helping to undergird other leaders. They agreed, with fear and trembling, to take the leadership of the church.

Mary Anne and I took time to meet with every family in our congregation to share with them the prophetic background for the change. The congregation was supportive of our move, and not one family left the church during this transition.

God does make all things beautiful in His time. Making a significant geographical and ministerial change was no small undertaking. It required the utmost care. Over the years, I have seen many people misjudge the timing of a God-willed event. Such missteps can be costly. Moses began sensing his call as deliverer of Israel years before God had everything in place, and his eagerness resulted in disaster (see Exodus 2:11-15).

In addition to handing over the leadership of the church, we had to sell our home. We tried to sell in the summer, so we could be in North Carolina by the beginning of the school year for our youngest son, but selling our house was also a walk of faith. We had no real offers, so it was difficult not to panic.

We also had to purchase a house in North Carolina. At the time, MorningStar was near the airport, but we had heard it was going to soon move to an unknown location. So, we prayed. We relentlessly asked God to show us where to move, so our commute would not be far from this unknown location. If God could tell David where to defeat the Philistines before they arrived near the mulberry trees, God could tell us the exact location to buy a house in Charlotte before MorningStar moved (see II Samuel 5:23-25).

The Scripture we received was Isaiah 35:2, where the Lord said the desert **"shall blossom abundantly and rejoice, even with joy and singing. The glory of Lebanon shall be given to it, the excellence of Carmel and Sharon. They shall see the glory of the Lord, the excellency of our God."**

The real estate map of Charlotte at the time was configured like a pie with numbered pie sections. After the Lord brought that to our minds, we learned that section five, the prophetic number of God's grace, bordered on Carmel and

Sharon Roads! This was where we were to live. The next time we were in Charlotte, we found a bank-owned home in section five, only seven miles from the future home of MorningStar, and bought it. God is so good! He will speak and even give you specific directions.

So, now we owned a home in North Carolina, but our house in New Jersey had not yet sold. At the time, real estate prices were rising, so we prayed earnestly for a buyer and explicitly for a bidding war between two buyers. That is exactly what happened. Our home sold later than we anticipated, but for a much higher price than we were asking—in a bidding war. Through God's goodness, we could spend one more Thanksgiving and Christmas with our family, then we were off to North Carolina by the new year!

One notable moment in this transition was our sendoff party hosted by the church. Years earlier, we were ushered out of town with people cursing us as we left. In this second sendoff, people were blessing us and our future endeavors. The church had been restored, the people were healed, and they knew their purpose. Through that, God had also restored our reputation. What a difference it makes when God is both **"the author and finisher of our faith" (see Hebrews 12:2)**. He is indeed a restorer.

11

Prophetic Markers

There are large movements within the church that are suspicious of the gifts of the Spirit. And some church leaders are even hostile toward the gift of prophecy. In I Corinthians 14, Paul exhorted us to earnestly desire spiritual gifts, especially prophecy (see I Corinthians 14:1, 39).

As I look back over my season of loss and restoration, prophecy played a vital role in giving me hope, comfort, and encouragement. In fact, I can confidently say that without those gifts operating in my life, I would not have seen God restore our losses. That is not to say that God cannot restore a person who does not actively have ongoing prophetic direction in their lives, only that prophecy was and still is vitally important in my life.

To understand the meaning of these prophetic words we receive, we must use the same methods we use to interpret Scripture. First, we *observe* what the Scripture is saying to the people of that time. Second, we endeavor to *interpret* the meaning of the Scripture. And third, we search for the *application* of those Scriptures to our lives—observation, interpretation, application.

Prophecy does not hold the same weight as the written, infallible Word of God. However, a true prophetic word given for edification, exhortation, and comfort is a proceeding word from the Lord and should be highly valued (see I Corinthians 14:3). So, for us to draw the most from a prophetic word, the same process of observation, interpretation, and application must be followed.

Let me explain how this process played a pivotal role in my life. In chapter one, I described the season of difficulty that surrounded my resignation. When I resigned, the judgments I made about my life were greatly influenced by the words spoken over me by my leaders. This led to confusion concerning my calling and purpose. Because I had placed these men in such high esteem, it was a real battle not to believe them.

One of the blessings of prophetic ministry is that it can identify false judgments and word curses. Such false judgments and word curses can have great influence in steering people's lives in the wrong direction. Word curses are reckless, hurtful words spoken by people who influence our lives. Such words can limit and even prevent people from walking in their destinies. The gift of prophecy played a key role in freeing me from the prison and paralysis of those word curses.

At pivotal moments along my journey, God continued to shed light on His direction for me through key prophetic words. I believe one reason the gifts of the Spirit and especially prophecy are attacked is because these critical words can be so powerfully lifegiving and lifesaving.

Shortly after I resigned, my wife and I decided to retreat to Florida to try and get our feet back under us. A ministry friend who was sympathetic to our circumstances suggested we stop to visit a "father-type pastor" who might encourage us. I marveled at the grace and kindness of this man to minister to someone he had never met. When we arrived, a prophet by the name of Jim Laffoon was with him. As soon as we walked into the man's home, Jim's prophetic antennas were activated.

Jim said he saw three knife wounds in my back that led to my decision to leave the ministry. Indeed, there were three principal people who played a vital role in my resignation. These three individuals twisted words I had spoken to them in unguarded moments to build a case as to why I was unqualified for ministry. Jim knew nothing about the circumstances surrounding my resignation. But here the Lord had not only identified but in great measure had also adjusted my perspective regarding the judgments of those leaders. The illustration of the backstabbing betrayal spoke deeply to me.

During my years of playing sports, I understood the importance of teamwork. Loyalty to one's teammates and covering their mistakes were vital to team chemistry. My time serving in the military also reinforced this. To stab a fellow team member or soldier in the back was a low blow. That prophetic choice of words and symbolism spoke volumes to me that this was something against God's code of conduct. This word picture also gave me a deeper connection to what the Lord must have felt when Judas betrayed Him.

Throughout the entire ordeal, I made a silent pledge that I would never bring that sort of pain on someone else. At times, I watched as other pastors and leaders experienced similar heartaches. Much later, I realized my experience of pain was part of my preparation as director of MorningStar Fellowship of Ministries. Even while on staff at Morning-Star, this spirit again raised its ugly head. But the fact that I had been down that road before served me well during those trying times.

Jim's prophetic words were a major marker in my life. I did not realize it then, but this word of knowledge gave me future insight to help many others. Identifying this wound became key to my freedom over word curses pronounced over my life. This prophetic marker was monumental.

Then there was Bob Jones' word: "Tom, you have breathed in some bad air, and the Lord is working that out of your system." In time, as I reflected on Bob's words, I gained more insight into their full meaning and how this applied to my life. Some prophetic words have what I call "an unfolding life cycle" that extends into the future.

Perhaps you've read a Scripture a hundred times before, but suddenly when you read it the hundred and first time, you see something you never saw before. Through prayer, I realized that some of the "bad air" I had breathed were certain practices and traditions within our movement God had to work out of my system. I also realized if I ever went back into ministry, I would need what is called in the technological world "a systems upgrade." This prophetic word came at a very important time in my life and helped me through the restoration process.

Zacharias, the father of John the Baptist, was a priest within the religious system of his day. John was raised in that system, but there came a day when John not only left that system but also became critical of that system. John had learned all he was going to learn from that system. Some people's journeys take them on similar paths. I also found myself thrust out of a system. I then had to realize that some of what I had learned was how *not* to do things.

Over the years, I have observed people who have become embittered by their church experiences and leaders. Criticisms that come from deep woundings and offenses are not only nonproductive but also defile many. John's critique was different. John knew the ax had been laid to the root of that system and that God was preparing to give birth to a new system (see Matthew 3:10). John was attempting to remove people from a system that would eventually incur the wrath of God. **"Who warned you to flee from the wrath to come?" (see Matthew 3:7)**

"Bad air" had many implications in the system in which I was raised. Our system was significantly influenced by a religious spirit. To command our kids to walk in "holiness," we established a "no dating" policy and a "no makeup" policy for girls in our K-12 school. The application of this rule resulted in overreach into families' lives. Such rules and guidelines should be established in individual homes, not by church leaders.

Another area needing serious adjustment was the women's ministry. It was the policy of our movement that women could speak in public settings but only to other women and only on women's topics, like "how to be a good wife and mother." To further complicate the issue, only older women could speak in these settings, and "older women" was defined as thirty-eight years or older!

It's almost laughable today, but at the same time sad that we adhered to such policies. Yet, these were all examples of how "bad air" had found its home in my life and ministry. This had legalism as its root, of which Jesus warned His disciples:

> **"'How is it you do not understand that I did not speak to you concerning bread?—but to beware of the leaven of the Pharisees and Sadducees.'**
> **"Then they understood that He did not tell them to beware of the leaven of bread, but of the doctrine of the Pharisees and Sadducees"** (Matthew 16:11-12).

As we began to loosen these restrictions in our ministry, it provoked a response from the religious spirit—and our ministry headquarters. I have heard it said that the church today is more influenced by the religious spirit than the Holy Spirit. I shudder to think this is true. Certainly, religious spirits and the legalistic policies they establish find comfortable places to operate when leaders with even the best intentions are given control over people. In our system, we had a term for conduct that was considered outside the traditional bounds of holiness. We called it, "flying below the radar" when we chose not to adhere to strict religious policies.

As Mary Anne and I "sat on the bench" in Charlotte, we were exposed to a new system of ministry. Rick often said that he enjoyed provoking the religious spirit. We had a front row seat watching Rick do just that. It was both entertaining and inspiring. We were taught a new ministry paradigm. Bob's word helped us breathe the fresh air of godly freedom that belongs to God's people.

Another word given by Jim Laffoon came when we had been in Charlotte for months and my job search was proving unsuccessful. In my private prayer time, when I would ask the Lord where I was to look for work, I would consistently hear the word, "Wait." However, I had reasoned that I could *not* wait, because I had a wife and family to support. The longer my unsuccessful job search lingered, the more worried and distressed I became.

As I walked into a meeting in Raleigh, North Carolina, Jim came over to me and gave me a stinging word, "What God has intended for a time of rest, you have turned into a time of worry." Again, guilty as charged! Jim's words reinforced the "wait" word the Lord had been speaking to me for months. Waiting was also counterintuitive when I had no job or income, but Jim's words gave me confidence that the Lord wanted me to dial down. The application of this word was to rest, which became another key to my future freedom.

Our move to New Jersey was also surrounded by several prophetic words given by individuals who did not know our situation. "Tom, you are not the man for this job, but unpack your winter clothes because you're moving back to New Jersey," and "Tom, you will be going back to a people, and you will be a lifeboat, life preserver, and lighthouse for them."

These words were followed by circumstantial confirmations, like my brother-in-law offering me a job which required me to relocate to New Jersey. Of course, there is a legitimate caution to being led simply by prophetic words. While we were receiving these prophetic words, we were also being responsible to "test" or prove these words in our spirits. **"Do not quench the Spirit. Do not despise prophecies. Test all things; hold fast what is good" (I Thessalonians 5:19-21).**

Through all the twists and turns, God was faithful to personally give us direction through either dreams or words spoken to our hearts alerting us to our path.

Though we had clear words of direction, we were not always excited about taking those next steps. Mary Anne was reluctant and even resistant to the idea of returning to New Jersey. After all, this had been a place of great distress and personal rejection, and many were glad when we left. So, although these prophetic words were clear, it required great faith and obedience to move forward. God is a rewarder of faith and obedience, and these were the steps we needed to take along our road to restoration.

Even the prophetic direction we received to return to MorningStar proved to be difficult. Kingsley Fletcher identified my wife and me by name and even encouraged Rick to invite us to join his team. This was the Lord. And for that word to be further reinforced by John Paul Jackson was clearly God. Other prophetic words from visiting ministers made it unmistakably God!

However, I would be remiss not to tell you what came after those amazing prophetic words. I already told you two and a half years prior to receiving those words, Mary Anne and I began praying aloud about change coming to our ministry. This included the prayer of Jabez to enlarge our territory. We not only prayed this prayer but also used Bruce Wilkinson's book *The Prayer of Jabez* as a spiritual roadmap to our breakthrough. In fact, I believe those prayers of agreement had an impact on those prophetic words we received. When Daniel realized that the change was coming to release God's people back to their homeland, he took an active role through prayer and fasting to aid the process (see Daniel 9:2-19).

Significant prophetic words that give life-changing direction can be released through focused prayer, fasting, and intercession. I believe God wants us to release more words of such magnitude as we fervently press into the heart of God (see James 5:16).

As I write, I can hear the thoughts of many readers wishing they could receive similar prophetic input. One key for me receiving solid, ongoing, prophetic input was finding my tribe. In the Old Testament, the nation of Israel was organized into twelve tribes. Each tribe had special, unique gifts. Likewise, there are distinct giftings in the church today.

As my spiritual life matured, something began to develop inside me that I could not articulate. A part of this development did not quite fit within my movement. It was like I was speaking a different language and not being understood. When I began to read Rick Joyner's book *The Harvest*, I finally found someone who was playing the same sheet music. In time, God opened doors to develop relationships, and we settled at MorningStar. I finally found a people who spoke my language. Still, the path to my destiny, like Joseph, was full of twists and turns. When I developed relationships with this new tribe, I received most of the important prophetic direction for my life.

Some relationships are important for us to recognize and maintain. When Nehemiah set out to restore and rebuild Jerusalem, he identified who to and *not* to build with. The people we are *not* to build with are not bad or evil people; they just don't have the call to complement the kingdom purposes God has ordained for our lives. We all need to be sensitive enough to know who these key kingdom relationship people are, because it is through these special connections that God's kingdom is advanced.

The night before Jesus named His apostolic team of twelve, He spent all night in prayer. Likewise, when we choose our team, we need to carefully recognize, develop, and maintain those relationships. It is within these relationships that great ground is taken. It is also where we find the most focused attacks of the enemy.

When MorningStar was established, Rick Joyner realized that many likeminded leaders did not have connections with each other. To fill that void, MorningStar Fellowship of Ministries began. The vision was to create an atmosphere where leaders and those called to ministry could connect and draw upon each other's gifts to strengthen and stand with one another through good times and bad.

As of this writing, that division of MorningStar is twenty-seven years old, and as director of the Fellowship of Ministries, I have witnessed this vision being fulfilled.

Time and again, I have witnessed leaders who needed to hear important words from God and a team of people who held them up in prayer, or simply came alongside them through difficult times. I have watched as ministries and families have been saved, while others have stood with them through critical moments.

As you study the Bible, you don't have to dig deep to understand the importance of relationships. Along with my MorningStar University students, I have studied the entire New Testament and book of Proverbs, while also surveying the Old Testament, to learn about key relationships.

The Bible has clear instructions on how we are to interact with one another as families, husbands and wives, parents and children, and employers and employees. All relationships and corresponding responsibilities require different responses. If we look a little deeper into these relationships, we will find relationships that are authorized and ordained by God with God-ordained kingdom purposes attached to them. **"God sets the solitary in families" (see Psalm 68:6)**. As Director of MorningStar Fellowship of Ministries, I have watched this network grow to more than four hundred members.

People often face difficult decisions, and while these can be difficult crossroads, most leaders simply want to follow the Lord. Those who have been most supported through trying or distressing times have developed friendships with other ministers who can speak into their lives. Sadly, I have also witnessed some who have stumbled in ministry, and these missteps were further compounded when no one was there to stand with them or hold them up. Ecclesiastes clearly speaks to this: **"Two are better than one, because they have a good reward for their labor. For if they fall, one will lift up his companion. But woe to him who is alone when he falls, for he has no one to help him up"** (Ecclesiastes 4:9-10).

As I looked back over my years of hardship, how I wished someone had been there to speak a prophetic word to me in my exact moment of crisis. That happened later, and I am eternally grateful for that. But as we built MFM, I remembered my season of distress, and it was with that in mind that we constructed the prophetic councils to be available to our members.

Upon request, we assemble teams of four to six experienced prophetic people who will pray and ask the Lord for counsel for the one who has requested it. The team is not told anything about the person for which they are praying. In these Zoom meetings, the team ministers prophetically, and the results are always beyond expectation. Many relationships have also been developed through these councils. I liken these prophetic councils to specially trained military teams that are sent out into difficult circumstances to rescue people in distress. The fruit from these councils has been outstanding.

Often, we are approached at MorningStar by people who desperately want a prophetic word. Whether at MorningStar Fellowship Church in Fort Mill or at one of our many MorningStar Conferences, we have prophetic teams who are trained and ready to minister to people who want prophetic ministry. These words have also been lifechanging.

To summarize, the prophetic words which were given to me played a key role in my restoration. Many of these words came from relationships, which have been vital to my life. I encourage you to also be sensitive and recognize the key individuals and divine connections God brings into your life, so you too can advance His kingdom purposes.

12

Don't Settle

In Numbers 32, there is a clear illustration of God's people settling for less than God's best. The designated boundaries God promised to Abraham were on the other side of the Jordan. However, after forty years of wandering, Israel had already conquered the land of Gilead, and some of the tribes saw this land as a desirable place to raise children, build homes, and allow their cattle to graze.

When the leaders of Ruben, Gad, and half the tribe of Manasseh approached Moses with their request to settle, he was not favorable to their request. Still, Moses yielded on one condition: they must continue to fight with the rest of the nation in the upcoming battles. Moses' objection to their desire to settle prematurely sent a discouraging message to the rest of the nation. While setting up residence on the other side of the Jordan may have been appealing after a long season of struggle, it did not convey a victorious overcoming message.

Likewise, after the choices I had made, the last thing I wanted to do was send a message of discouragement to others. Now that things were going well for me and my family, I did not want to settle. I remembered the advice one of my mentors gave me shortly after I entered ministry: "Tom, when heaven looks down on your life, the report you want the angels to take back to the Father is that you incentivized others to serve God with a heart of passion." I have since endeavored to heed that godly advice.

After my second church plant in New Jersey, and after we started to get our feet back under us, I began to feel the whisper of God in my spirit that there was more He desired from us than just to heal our brokenness. I could hear the cry of the broken and desperate and understood God wanted to use the heartache we had experienced to heal others. We had more work to do.

Moses himself was another illustration of not walking in the full plan of God. There were powerful messages from the life of Moses that spoke to me.

Numbers 20 records great unrest among God's people for a lack of water. The instruction the Lord gave to Moses was to speak to the rock to bring forth water. It should be noted this event occurred about thirty-eight years after they entered the wilderness. Moses calling God's people "rebels" was likely an indication of accumulated ministry frustration. However, Moses' momentary unrighteous anger of striking the rock instead resulted in him not entering the land of promise.

As I went back into ministry, I could not let the years of conflict dictate how I related to many of the same people who had once maligned me. Bob Jones once gave me a very descriptive prophetic exhortation, which spoke volumes to me. Bob picked up on some irritation I was experiencing toward a particularly troubling person. He looked me square in the eye and said, "You have to remember to flush!"

At this juncture, Bob was also feeling pressure from many different ministries and people. Not to mention the pressures he felt from answering calls from all over the world from people in crisis. Yet, Bob seemed to have perfected this practice of "flushing." Now, looking back over Bob's life, one of my most significant memories was the kindness and peace that emanated from him.

We are all familiar with the phrase, "I am processing." Jacob's son, Joseph, is a profound example of a man who "processed" well. Genesis 45 records how Joseph not only released his brothers from their painful misdeeds but also understood the unseen hand of God working behind those painful circumstances to preserve their lives. God indeed intended everything for good. Joseph also "flushed" well.

I have often reflected on the unpredictable course God allowed me to take. When we returned to New Jersey, there was much "flushing" to do, yet even then, we barely realized the full fruit that was produced during that difficult season. God's destiny was woven into every step we took.

Another illustration from David's life powerfully exhorts us to take every inch of ground God intends for us. Again, David dealt with boundaries, which God designated for conquest to walk in his full destiny. To understand this phase of David's life, we must grasp the history of David and the Jebusites.

David's life sends a different message to those who have chosen to settle for less than what God has designated for them. A quick review of his life will help us more fully appreciate this.

Around the age of seventeen, David was anointed by the prophet Samuel as King of Israel. The next thirteen years were completely opposite of a kingly role and anything but peaceful. David was chased by Saul, completely unaware that these were years of testing and preparation. David was just trying to survive. I can relate well to living in survival mode. Perhaps you can also.

After a long, arduous journey, the headwinds of adversity which had blown fiercely against David dramatically shifted. Saul's death is recorded in I Samuel 31:1-13. When David was thirty, this period of trial came to an end as 432,000 warriors gathered at Hebron to make David king (see I Chronicles 12).

Here again we must grasp the history of the nation of Israel and the Jebusites and the importance of Jerusalem. When Joshua invaded the promised land, he defeated five kings, including the king of the Jebusites or king of Jerusalem (see Joshua 10). However, the defeat of the Jebusites did not prevent them from reoccupying their land. From the time of Joshua's invasion to the time of David (approximately 400 years), Jerusalem remained in the hands of the Jebusites.

Thus, some critical areas which God had designated for His people remained strongholds of Israel's enemies. Jerusalem, the stronghold of the Jebusites, came into full view after David's years of testing and opposition. David could not allow this stronghold, which was God's designated territory, to remain in the hands of His enemies. It took a man after God's own heart, who had both the wisdom and the courage to secure the city and secure Israel's ultimate destiny. Thus, Jerusalem would become a city of supreme importance to Israel, and since David captured it and made it his own stronghold, it would be called the City of David.

Hopefully, like David, you have emerged from your years of testing and have seen some victories along the way, but there may yet be strongholds for you to bring down. As New Testament believers, we can draw much inspiration from David's determination to bring down a longstanding enemy stronghold and reoccupy God's designated territory.

During the years of conflict between David and Saul, the Jebusites grew confident that their stronghold could never be taken by a fractured nation of Israel. This condescension continued even after David was made king at Hebron.

From those observing your seasons of weakness, the same condescending attitudes that David endured from the Jebusites may come your way. Likewise, when you emerge from your season of hardship, you may face similar challenges. After more than forty years in ministry, I have observed numerous people wanting to be close to me when I experience success. We call these "fair-weather" friends. Conversely, few desired to be next to me in my season of hardship.

Still, I took note of those who stood by me in my season of hardship, when most of my "friends" drifted away. It's also important to note those who drift away, not for vengeance's sake, but to note those who remained as truly those with which to rebuild. Those who remained when the dust cleared were true friends.

> **From that time many of His disciples went back and walked with Him no more.**
> **Then Jesus said to the twelve, "Do you also want to go away?"**
> **But Simon Peter answered Him, "Lord, to whom shall we go? You have the words of eternal life" (John 6:66-68).**

> **A friend loves at all times, and a brother is born for adversity (Proverbs 17:17).**

On David's deathbed, he remembered three people: Joab, Shimei, and Barzillai. David warned Solomon about Joab and Shimei, but after all of David's years of war and challenges, the only person David remembered in a positive way was Barzillai, who stood with him through his season of adversity.

Barzillai came to David's aid when David's son, Absalom, forced him out of Jerusalem. Barzillai's life was a true pattern of godly friendship. I have heard Rick Joyner say that relationships can be like the stock market; the best time to buy is when the price is low. People you help during their lowest point are the most grateful. Barzillai's help to David did not go unnoticed. We should follow his example. And, as noted, Rick Joyner helped me and my family during the lowest point of our lives, and we remain forever grateful.

Jerusalem was eventually where the temple of God was built. Jerusalem was also where the Israelites were called to gather three times each year for feasts. This was David's ultimate place of destiny. David did not settle for an incomplete victory, nor can we.

When Joash, King of Israel, came before Elisha seeking counsel about the enemies on his doorstep, Elisha instructed him to do something that speaks to us today (see II Kings 13:14-19). Joash was instructed to strike the ground with the arrows of deliverance. However, Joash only struck the ground three times, which angered Elisha because striking the ground only three times meant limited victories. Likewise, the scope and extent of our victories are in our hands. We must not settle for limited victories. And likewise, the stronghold of our Jerusalem is before us and must be taken.

The following Scriptures and chart on the next page illustrate David's challenges through age thirty-seven.

David was thirty years old when he began to reign, and he reigned forty years.

In Hebron he reigned over Judah seven years and six months, and in Jerusalem he reigned thirty-three years over all Israel and Judah.

And the king and his men went to Jerusalem against the Jebusites, the inhabitants of the land, who spoke to David, saying, "You shall not come in here; but the blind and the lame will repel you," thinking, "David cannot come in here."

Nevertheless David took the stronghold of Zion (that is, the City of David).

Now David said on that day, "Whoever climbs up by way of the water shaft and defeats the Jebusites (the lame and the blind, who are

Overview of David's Early Life

Consider the life of David:

- David is annointed king by Samuel, the most powerful religious leader of his time
- David kills Goliath, which provokes Saul to jealousy
- Saul seeks to kill David and hires three thousand assassins to perform the job

David is anointed by Samuel					All Israel gathers to King David at Hebron	
Age 17					**Age 30**	**Age 37**
Bethlehem					Hebron	Jerusalem
1 Sam. 16:1-13					*1 Chron. 12:38*	*2 Sam. 5:4-10*
1068 BC					1055 BC	1048 BC

Saul seeks to kill David	David flees to the wilderness	Mighty men join ranks with David	David refuses to kill Saul	David's men seek to kill David

hated by David's soul), he shall be chief and captain." Therefore they say, "The blind and the lame shall not come into the house."

Then David dwelt in the stronghold, and called it the City of David. And David built all around from the Millo and inward.

So David went on and became great, and the Lord God of hosts was with him"
(II Samuel 5:4-10).

Note that David took down the stronghold of Jerusalem, but also *how* he took that stronghold. To take the city, David's men went through the sewer system. These tunnels provided a flow of water into and through the city, but by the time the water exited the city, it was filled with waste. It was through these tunnels that David's men captured the city and brought down this stronghold.

This message is clear: to bring down strongholds and arrive at our ultimate destiny, we may first have to go through some nasty things, including our own "stinking thinking" we have embraced. And while these strongholds may appear impenetrable, God will give us keys to bring down places the enemy has held far too long. Many of us have become so familiar with negative patterns of living that have held us back, we no longer recognize our own "stinking thinking."

The strongholds David faced were very different from those New Testament believers face. For us, demonic strongholds may be a habitual negative thought pattern. These negative patterns can gain entrance through critical words or word curses spoken over us by influential people. In time, these words can hover over our minds and crystallize themselves into our belief systems about ourselves. Such strongholds can be further exacerbated by principalities over regions which fill spiritual atmospheres with demonic powers. The enemy can then put the thought in our minds that our problems are too strong to conquer. Unless we combat these negative thought patterns, we can become imprisoned to such false beliefs.

Many of us have inherited both good and bad traits from previous generations. Strongholds in our family lines are often left for us to overcome. We must overcome these negative habits and life patterns that troubled our fathers. Remember, if we will not drive out our enemies from the land, they will become pricks in our eyes and thorns in our sides.

> **"But if you do not drive out the inhabitants of the land from before you, then it shall be that those whom you let remain shall be irritants in your eyes and thorns in your sides, and they shall harass you in the land where you dwell.**
> **"Moreover it shall be that I will do to you as I thought to do to them" (Numbers 33:55-56).**

Such strongholds can manifest themselves in depression, anxiety, bitterness, recurring unbelief, uncontrolled anger, worthlessness, constant feelings of rejection or inferiority, expecting continual failure, perceiving correction as rejection, perfectionism, or the constant need to control.

When I took a sober look at my own life, I discovered inferiority had a stronghold on me. Then I discovered it had a stronghold on many of God's people today. This judgment that led to an inferiority complex greatly contributed to the length and depth of my depression. I was also encouraged by the fact that many of our great heroes of faith like Moses, Jeremiah, and David experienced similar struggles and were able to overcome them.

Over the years, I have observed what career counselors recommend for those seeking employment. Candidates are often advised to put together a "brag sheet" to talk openly about their life's accomplishments.

Before you quote a Scripture about how we are to humble ourselves under the mighty hand of God that He may exalt us in due season, let's put this in context with another biblical illustration. In Exodus 3, God called Moses to his life's purpose, but after Moses spent years in the wilderness going through God's "stripping" process, he was no longer confident that he could fulfill God's purpose. Moses' response was anything but a "brag sheet." In fact, his response angered the Lord. After my public stripping, my response was much like Moses', "I can't do this!"

We must all learn how to properly respond to new seasons in our lives. Moses needed to get in step with God, I needed to get in step with God, and you may need to get in step with God to see His plans unfold. **"For I know the plans that I have for you," declares the Lord, "plans for prosperity and not for disaster, to give you a future and a hope" (Jeremiah 29:11).** God's plans for you are good. He wants you to have hope for your future. Those are *His* words, and God is not a man that He should lie (see Numbers 23:19).

Your "brag sheet" may look something like this: I have been humbled by the mighty hand of God. I have been through a public stripping. I have been through a furnace of affliction, and like Peter, I have failed, but I will not make the same mistake again. Paul wrote about his afflictions and what qualified him for ministry:

> "Seeing that many boast according to the flesh, I also will boast.
>
> "For you put up with fools gladly, since you yourselves are wise!
>
> "For you put up with it if one brings you into bondage, if one devours you, if one takes from you, if one exalts himself, if one strikes you on the face.
>
> "To our shame I say that we were too weak for that! But in whatever anyone is bold—I speak foolishly—I am bold also.
>
> "Are they Hebrews? So am I. Are they Israelites? So am I. Are they the seed of Abraham? So am I.
>
> "Are they ministers of Christ?—I speak as a fool—I am more: in labors more abundant, in stripes above measure, in prisons more frequently, in deaths often.
>
> "From the Jews five times I received forty stripes minus one.
>
> "Three times I was beaten with rods; once I was stoned; three times I was shipwrecked; a night and a day I have been in the deep;
>
> "in journeys often, in perils of waters, in perils of robbers, in perils of my own countrymen, in perils of the Gentiles, in perils

**in the city, in perils in the wilderness, in perils in
the sea, in perils among false brethren;**
   **"in weariness and toil, in sleeplessness often,
in hunger and thirst, in fastings often, in cold
and nakedness—**
   **"besides the other things, what comes upon
me daily: my deep concern for all the churches"
(II Corinthians 11:18-29).**

Everyone's brag sheet looks different. Paul said the Corinthians boasted about their fleshly accomplishments, though it was really the grace of God which enabled them to accomplish those things. Ultimately, only God's approval matters. Paul listed all the hardships and failures he endured as a list of qualifications for ministry. Self-commendation or the praise of men counts for nothing.

Not knowing who we are or Whose we are is tragic. Identity theft happens when personal information is breached or stolen. *Spiritual* identity theft happens when knowledge of who we are and Whose we are is lost or stolen. Identity theft is one of the leading crimes on earth today, which should speak to us prophetically.

The woman in the Song of Solomon did not have a clear understanding of how heaven viewed her. Many of God's people today have a murky view of their God-given potential, and the enemy has been working overtime to keep us hobbling under this cloud of inferiority. But for those who are willing to fight and bring down these generational strongholds, for those who are willing to pray great prayers of faith, the land God has designated for us awaits the champions inside us to awaken. God is calling us to rise and meet the challenge of this hour.

I remember a young man who worked as an apprentice carpenter for my father-in-law's general contracting firm. He worked in finished carpentry with very expensive trim work. His instructions were to "measure twice and cut once." However, in his impatience to finish his work by the end of each day, he neglected to follow these instructions. Sure enough, the expensive trim work was ruined. He was devastated, but as a Christian believer he needed to own his mistakes.

He met with my father-in-law expecting to be laid off for his carelessness. As he sheepishly approached him and apologized for his error, my father-in-law's response was classic: "Well son, if I let you go, you will go down the street to my rival company. They will hire you and receive the benefit of you never making that mistake again. They will get the benefit of the costly mistake my company has paid for. Now get back to work!"

Moses' sense of inferiority was predictable but not acceptable in God's sight. The sense of inferiority I carried from my beatings was also predictable but not acceptable to the Lord. Likewise, the sense of inferiority that much of the church carries today is not acceptable. Here is one of the keys to breaking this stronghold in my life.

Jabez is an interesting Bible character. Jabez's mother bore him in pain, and his name, which means "pain," reflected that experience. His story is recorded in I Chronicles 4:9-10: **"Now Jabez was more honorable than his brothers, and**

his mother called his name Jabez, saying, 'Because I bore him in pain.' And Jabez called on the God of Israel saying, 'Oh, that You would bless me indeed, and enlarge my territory, that Your hand would be with me, and that You would keep me from evil, that I may not cause pain!' So God granted him what he requested."

Jabez did not want the rest of his life to be defined by pain. He did not want people to remember a painful experience when they heard his name. I, too, did not want my kids to remember only the difficult days of their dad's life when they thought of me. Instead, like Jabez, I wanted to be defined as having an extraordinary life. I believe you also would like your life to be defined not by the painful times you lived through, but by the victories you have achieved. No one aspires to live an insignificant life.

Bruce Wilkinson's book *The Prayer of Jabez* contains powerful prayers which were transformational in our lives and can be transformational in your life also. We adapted several thoughts and phrases from the book to fit our prayer style and life circumstances. I encourage you to get this book and adapt it to your prayer life as well. Here are several prayers we prayed:

- *Lord, I reach for an extraordinary life, the kind You promise. Lord, give me a bigger vision for my life. I want nothing but Your fullest blessing for my life. I want Your plenty.*

- *Lord, show me where to throw my energy, passion, and training. I jump into the river of Your grace and power to carry me along. I want Your plan that will sweep me into the profoundly important, and the satisfying life You have for me.*

- *I ask for more and more again. Father, bless me and bless me a lot. Impart supernatural favor. I ask for nothing more and nothing less than what You want for me. I cry out for the unlimited goodness that only You have the power to know about or can give to me.*

- *I throw myself into the river of Your will, power, and purposes for me. I want to be wholly immersed in what You are trying to do in me, through me, and around me, for Your glory. I want a life marked by miracles!*

- *I ask for Your power to accomplish great things. I pray for exactly what You desire, and I ask for the unhindered forces of heaven to accomplish Your perfect will through me.*

- *Lord, there is no limit to Your goodness. I ask for blessing here today among us.*

- *Impart supernatural favor. I cry out for the wonderful, unlimited goodness that only You have the power to know about or can give to me. The Lord's blessing is our greatest wealth, all our work adds nothing to it (see Proverbs 10:22).*

- *The blessing of the Lord makes rich, and He adds no sorrow to it.*

- *As Moses asked, "Show us Your glory" (see Exodus 33:18), I also ask for a more intimate understanding of You.*

- *Your bounty is limited only by me, not by Your resources, power, or willingness to give. I refuse to allow any obstacle, person, or opinion to loom larger than God's nature. And Your nature is to bless.*

- *Help me to make a mark for the God of Israel!*

- *Enlarge my territory! Everything You have put under my care, Lord, take it and enlarge it! Take and increase the value of my work, my personal businesses, my wealth, the work You have granted me and allowed me to prosper in; take it and enlarge it.*

- *Give me significant opportunities to touch individual lives, the community around me, and the larger world for Your glory. Enlarge those opportunities and give me creative ideas and ventures.*

- *I ask in earnest, I beg You to give me more influence and responsibility with which to honor You. Bring opportunities and people into my path. Let me experience the tremendous thrill of You carrying me along as I am doing Your will. Let me be like John and Peter who were given the very words to say the moment they needed them.*

- *Oh, that You would bless me indeed and enlarge my border, and that Your hand might be with me, and that You would keep me from harm that it may not pain me.*

- *And God granted him what he requested (see I Chronicles 4:10).*

When Mary Anne and I began praying these prayers, we were pastoring a healthy but relatively small church. We loved the people but believed God had more for us to accomplish with the gifts and calling on our lives. When God answered those prayers, our opportunities in life and ministry enlarged beyond our expectations.

Jabez was not content to be defined by the pain that marked his past. When we examined the lives of Bible characters like Moses, David, and Joseph, they far underestimated the plan and the commission God had in mind for them. We can learn from these Bible heroes not to limit God by our limited vision.

As we prayed the above prayers on a consistent basis, God remapped our boundary lines. "Larger borders, an appointment to keep. I ask for a miracle! Help me to expand Your kingdom a lot. Lord, use me. Give me more ministry for You. Release miracles! Let heaven send the angels, resources, strength, and people I need."

The Bible teaches several ways to break strongholds:

1. In Matthew 16 and 18, we are given authority to bind and loose the activity of the devil. A prayer of agreement can have a powerful effect to conquer attempted demonic incursions.

2. Ephesians 6 teaches us to wrestle against principalities and powers by standing after putting on the whole armor of God. We are instructed to take up the shield of faith, put on the breastplate of righteousness, put on the helmet of salvation, and take

up the sword of the Spirit. All these tools are available to us in battle. I well remember using the shield of faith to quench the fiery darts of the wicked one.

3. **"But you, beloved, building up yourselves on your most holy faith, praying in the Holy Ghost, Keep yourselves in the love of God, looking for the mercy of our Lord Jesus Christ unto eternal life" (Jude 1:20-21 KJV).** Looking back, I remember the waves of dark clouds which came at me, but once I began responding with the regular practice of praying in the Spirit, I overcame those demonic powers.

We are exhorted in Scripture to cast down imaginations by placing guards over our hearts (see Proverbs 4:23). From our hearts flow the real issues of life. Many thoughts that come to us are exaggerations of the enemy who seeks to discourage us. **"For the weapons of our warfare are not carnal but mighty in God for pulling down strongholds, casting down arguments and every high thing that exalts itself against the knowledge of God, bringing every thought into captivity to the obedience of Christ" (II Corinthians 10:4-5).**

There are additional remedies to strongholds which have hung over family lines for generations. These stubborn strongholds can become such a part of our heritage that we barely even recognize them. They dwell in the shadows of our past, but we must free ourselves so the next generation can also be freed from these chains.

Isaiah 58:12 describes **"old waste places"** and **"foundations of many generations."** This verse describes ruined lives, but also carries the profound promise of rebuilding lives and old waste places. **"Those from among you shall build the old waste places; You shall raise up the foundations of many generations; and you shall be called the Repairer of the Breach, The Restorer of Streets to Dwell In"** (Isaiah 58:12).

To fully understand how this promise can be activated in the lives of many people, we must read it in its context:

> **"Is this not the fast that I have chosen: to loose the bonds of wickedness, to undo the heavy burdens, to let the oppressed go free, and that you break every yoke?**
>
> **"Is it not to share your bread with the hungry, and that you bring to your house the poor who are cast out; when you see the naked, that you cover him, and not hide yourself from your own flesh?"** (Isaiah 58:6-7)

Another way to release God's people into their greatest freedom is in Jesus' Sermon on the Mount. In the Beatitudes, Jesus gives great encouragement to people who have suffered abuse and defamation at the hands of others. The word of encouragement is, **"great is your reward in heaven"** **(see Matthew 5:12).**

However, we often overlook the second part of this sermon on how to *respond* to those who have mistreated us. I must admit I am still growing in this area.

> **"You have heard that it was said, 'You shall love your neighbor and hate your enemy.'**

"But I say to you, love your enemies, bless those who curse you, do good to those who hate you, and pray for those who spitefully use you and persecute you,

"that you may be sons of your Father in heaven; for He makes His sun rise on the evil and on the good, and sends rain on the just and on the unjust.

"For if you love those who love you, what reward have you? Do not even the tax collectors do the same?

"And if you greet your brethren only, what do you do more than others? Do not even the tax collectors do so?

"Therefore, you shall be perfect, just as your Father in heaven is perfect" (Matthew 5:43-48).

I recently heard a message by Joe Sweet, a pastor in California who struggled with negative feelings toward the people who had split his church. I also wrestled with deep feelings of resentment and anger toward close friends who had wounded me this way. In this pastor's account, he admitted wrestling with this and wanted to be released from those negative thoughts, which had built such a strong grip on him. However, after months of struggling, and in a momentary encounter, the Lord charted a path to freedom for him. He said, "I have not called you not to hate them; I have called you to love them."

What a profound word of wisdom for those who find themselves in the grip of such negative emotions. There are biblical solutions that can help us decouple ourselves from the pain that can grip our souls. Other Scriptures reinforce this direction for those who are caught in the wake of these emotions.

> **"Beloved, do not avenge yourselves, but rather give place to wrath; for it is written, 'Vengeance is Mine, I will repay,' says the Lord.**
> **"Therefore 'If your enemy is hungry, feed him; if he is thirsty, give him a drink; for in so doing you will heap coals of fire on his head.'**
> **"Do not be overcome by evil, but overcome evil with good" (Romans 12:19-21).**

With this new direction from the Lord, Joe sat down and wrote a kind note to the one who had split the church and enclosed a gift card for dinner. He continued this practice on random occasions. In time, as the pastor continued to pray for this person and send notes, the relationship was restored. Such restoration of troubled relationships is rarely easy. However, breaking this stubborn stronghold may indeed be our "Jerusalem" and ultimate destiny.

Isaiah 58 describes the spiritual condition of a people under bands of wickedness and heavy burdens of oppression. Isaiah's proposed solution was fasting. I have witnessed just such a grip being broken off people's minds through fasting. These fasts do not necessarily need to be forty days but should include regular intervals of focused prayer, fasting, and petitioning God for deliverance. Of course, if God has urged you to fast forty days, go for it. Some have likened such extended times of fasting to releasing a spiritual atomic bomb!

Some of the most memorable moments in my athletic career occurred when we defeated our archrivals. However, nothing can be compared to the exhilaration of defeating thought patterns that have dominated our families for generations.

> **"Behold, I have given you authority to tread upon serpents and scorpions, and over all the power of the enemy, and nothing shall injure you.**
> **"Nevertheless do not rejoice in this, that the spirits are subject to you, but rejoice that your names are recorded in heaven" (Luke 10:19-20 NASB).**

In Exodus, God told the Israelites that He would not drive their enemies out of the land all at once but little by little: **"I will not drive them out from before thee in one year; lest the land become desolate, and the beast of the field multiply against thee. By little and little I will drive them out from before thee, until thou be increased, and inherit the land" (Exodus 23:29-30 KJV).**

In *Lord of the Rings: The Fellowship of the Ring*, there is an illustration that may help us better understand how God wants us to break free from generational forces which have kept us settling for less than God's best. As Gandalf and his troop were being pursued by evil forces, Gandalf suddenly stopped, turned to face the enemy, and proclaimed with all the force he could muster, "You shall not pass!" Such is the intensity and determination required to break the enemy's grip, which has imprisoned God's people far too long. We cannot allow such strongholds to continue taking ground in our lives. Let's not settle for less. Instead, let's rise in this critical hour of history to take every inch of ground God has designated for us!

13

Another Perspective

By Mary Anne Hardiman

As I read over Tom's draft for this book, many thoughts came to mind. First and foremost was the grace of God which brought us through our "dark night of the soul." His grace is sufficient, but in this season, it was certainly tested.

For about five years, every Christmas was a trial. It was difficult to be "merry and bright" when there was upheaval in the church. About eight years after the founding of our church, some of our elders and deacons started stretching their spiritual muscles. As part of the leadership, they also wanted oversight of the church. Not to repeat the early chapters, but we had a difficult time transitioning these "teenagers" into "adulthood." There comes a time when those you have trained and raised need a voice, and if you deny them that voice and outlet, dissatisfaction, frustration, and even rebellion can creep in.

We had never experienced this before. Just like parenting, pastoring is on-the-job training. So, by the time we started hearing of "rumors of war," it was too late. Every message Tom had preached had already been inaccurately communicated to the church overseers. From that point on, we could do nothing right, as the atmosphere of the church grew extremely tense.

Frank Peretti's book *Piercing the Darkness* had just been released, and the entire congregation seemed immersed in it. Each Sunday, I had to brace myself just to show up among their critical gazes and conversations. I put on my best face, led worship, and managed the church office, yet family after family began to leave amid rumors of a church split. As in Frank Peretti's book, as I gazed around the sanctuary, I imagined demons perched in our thirty-five-foot ceilings, whispering discontent into the ears of our congregation. Sadly, only a few others made that connection.

Physically, the stress took its toll on me. I must have lost about fifteen pounds. Tom couldn't sleep. Many nights I could hear him downstairs in the living room crying as quietly as he could. What had he done? How could this have happened? We were trying to follow the Lord. How could we face the people? How could we tell his family what had happened after all these years of trying to be good witnesses? How did we fail? We felt disgraced.

I remember driving to my parents' house and talking with my mom. I cried bitterly. "How could this happen?" I asked her. "You know, Mom, I never experienced abuse in our family, but this abuse in the church is unbearable." My mom and dad were strong believers, but at the time my dad was in the fight of his life with Parkinson's Disease and skin cancer. Nevertheless, they were amazing encouragers. Nine months later, my dad went on to glory.

When Tom checked in to the hospital, my dad called me and gave us this Scripture: **"I have chosen you and not rejected you. 'Do not fear, for I am with you; do not anxiously look about you, for I am your God. I will strengthen you, surely, I will help you, surely I will uphold you with My righteous right hand'"** (see Isaiah 41:9-10 NASB).

We needed help and needed upholding. Yes, He has called us, but to what? Everything was being called into question. That is how the devil works. He causes us to doubt whether our calling and election is sure. He causes us to doubt our own self-worth. He tries to discourage us to the point that we want to give up.

There were times when I was driving my car, and the thought came to me, "Just drive off the road. It's easy! Just do it. You won't be in pain anymore." This was crazy! I had never had such thoughts, yet they came several times. In my mind, I responded each time, "I have three young children. There's no way I can do this!" Whether it was my Irish gumption or righteous indignation, I thought, "No way! I'm not going to give the devil the satisfaction of knowing he made me give up, and I'm certainly not going to give my enemies that satisfaction!" Maybe it was a combination of gumption *and* righteous indignation. Nevertheless, we limped on.

One of my sisters and her husband and baby moved in with us for a few months just to help. As a family, we were so dysfunctional. Our only saving grace was that our children were still young, and young children are resilient. I remember when my youngest son disobeyed, I couldn't even tell him his behavior was unacceptable. I just shrugged my shoulders. At that point, my brother-in-law had to step in and correct him. He and my sister helped whenever and wherever they could, supporting us, giving ear to our sorrows, and cooking and cleaning.

A few pastor friends had also come out one week at a time to stay with us and preach on Sundays. One of them drove from Ohio once a month just to preach for us. Others flew in from the West Coast or Utah to encourage us. They were so kind, but what a difficult time. We quickly realized we could not continue under these conditions. Each week, families continued leaving the church. The whispers grew louder, and our reputation was already in the tank. Finally, the day came when we had to resign.

Now what? How would we make a living? Life was so painful living in a city among those who wanted us out. Yet, this was my husband's hometown. By now the entire community had heard about Tom Hardiman, how his church had kicked him out, and how he was to blame. It was all our fault. I told my mom, "I could understand if Tom had committed adultery or taken the church's money, but this all happened because they said he was harsh?!" The punishment was cruel. We were deemed unfit to lead; we had fallen and were cast out. Wow, did it hurt!

When we finally stopped crying, I was frightened. Would my husband ever recover? He was just a shell of the man I had married. His self-confidence was completely gone. Tom had done construction work in the past. Should we fall back on that? What careers should we pursue? We had many questions and no answers.

Shortly after our resignation, we stayed at my other sister's home in Florida for a few weeks to gather our thoughts. A good friend in North Carolina also invited us to come and stay in Charlotte. He told us, "Come and be my associate pastor. I can't pay you, but I could use the help." Yet another friend invited us to their place in Oregon, but we didn't want to be too far from my parents while my father was ill. So, Charlotte was the better choice, and in the summer of 1991, we sold our house and moved south. It truly was God's providential hand leading us. Many times, in dire situations, the unseen hand of God leads us even into the unknown.

As Providence directed, we rented a house across the street from Robin and Donna McMillan. They are dear friends, and we are so grateful for their wise counsel and friendship. We later learned that Robin had gone through a similar situation with his previous church. Many mornings, Tom and Robin walked through the neighborhood, talking and praying together.

Robin knew Rick Joyner and invited the Joyners and us to his house for a barbecue, and that is how our connection with MorningStar began, though our journey was far from over. Rick began the Friday night School of the Spirit (SOS) meetings, which were a lifeline to us. The worship and preaching brought much hope.

One month after we moved to Charlotte, my dad passed on to glory. I told the Lord, "I can't take much more. Please make the pain stop." I continued to lose weight. I could barely keep food in me as the stress continued. Eventually, as the months progressed in Charlotte, the stress lessened, and we settled into our "new normal."

We continued going to our friend's church on Sundays and to MorningStar on Fridays. We were spiritually fed and grateful we did not have church responsibilities, which was a novel experience for us, since we had been senior church leaders all our married lives.

After two years of both of us unsuccessfully finding employment in Charlotte, we received a prophetic word to go back to New Jersey. By now, we had spent nearly all the equity from the sale of our home. What were we to do?

In January 1993, Tom received a call from my brother asking him to come back to New Jersey and work for his construction firm. The kids were still in school, so I convinced Tom the easiest thing would be for him to go to New Jersey, scout out an area to live, and let the kids and I finish the school year in Charlotte. Truthfully, I just needed more time away from the source of the pain. I loved my husband, but life was difficult. I thought this would give me more time to rest. It did not.

Our time in Charlotte was coming to an end, yet we had no idea where to go. However, I was convinced we could not go back to the same place where we had been kicked out. The safest place seemed to be near my family in Northern New Jersey, yet the prices of homes up there were ridiculous. So, our search shifted back to Central New Jersey.

I can smile now at how God led us. The only home we could afford was a former drug home, yes, in the town where we had been kicked out. Each member of the previous owner's family had been arrested for drugs. We cleaned up the home, slowly painted each room, ripped out the carpet, and eventually remodeled the home. A week after we moved in, a police car stopped in front of the house. The two policemen came, saw us cleaning, and thanked us for moving into the house which had been a regular stop on their circuit. They were relieved that a "normal" family would now be living there—little did they know!

The home had to be completely restored. Even the sheet-rock and insulation had to be removed from most rooms since the previous owners were smokers. The smell was pervasive. Each day as Tom drove to work and the kids went to school, with paintbrush in hand, I painted all the house trim, every window, every doorway. My cry to the Lord then was, "Lord, what are we doing back here? This is cruel. But Lord, I know You directed us here, so I will trust You, but please don't let me become bitter. Please take that from me."

I knew one of the final tests Jesus went through was to be offered wine mixed with gall on the cross to dull the pain. Gall was made from bitter herbs like wormwood and myrrh. He refused. He wanted nothing that would diminish the punishment of our sins as He became the substitute for our sins on the cross (see II Corinthians 5:21). Jesus bore the full brunt of God's wrath against sin. He did not accept an easier way out.

Gall signifies bitterness. At the end of our lives, or as we get older, many become disqualified because they accept the gall of life and allow bitterness to reside in them instead of refusing it. My heart's desire was not to become a bitter old woman just because of the trauma I had been through.

Our house became a picture of what the Lord was doing with us: renovating, removing the wounds, healing the battle scars, and releasing new hope for the future. God's ways are so much higher than ours (see Isaiah 55:9).

A Tale of Three Kings by Gene Edwards was another book we read during this time. Every Christian should read this book. Spoiler alert: the three kings were Saul, David, and Absalom.

We all know Saul was crazy. Only when David played the lyre did Saul become calm and in his right mind. Nevertheless, for years he pursued David and commissioned three thousand assassins against him.

Incredibly, David had a right heart toward Saul. He even called him "my father," and when he cut off a piece of Saul's robe, his heart convicted him. A few times, David's men wanted him to kill Saul when he was within reach, but David refused.

Absalom rose against his father, David. He drew the people away from their king because he wanted to rule them himself. Absalom was a rebel who took advantage of bad times to lead people away from their true king. Absalom betrayed his father.

We don't want to be a Saul or an Absalom. You may have a Saul in your life, or you may be tempted to become an Absalom, but of David God said, **"He is a man after My own heart" (see Acts 13:22)**. David was a different kind of king. He did not kill the family of his predecessor, but instead gave honor to the sons of Saul and of Jonathan, even inviting them to sit at his table.

In Genesis, Joseph was a type of the rejected, a beloved son of God. Even after Joseph was reunited with his brothers, they were unsure of his motives, for when their father, Jacob, passed, the brothers were afraid Joseph would repay them for the evil they did to him. Joseph said to his brothers, God had a plan in everything that happened to him: **"But as for you, you meant evil against me; but God meant it for good, in order to bring it about as it is this day, to save many people alive" (Genesis 50:20-21).**

Tom and I thought we would be in Trenton, New Jersey the rest of our lives. We thought this would be our church home where we would raise our kids and live happily ever after. How little we knew! God used our "dark night of the soul" to get us out of our comfort zone and bring us to our promised land. What man meant for evil, God used for His good. If we had never gone through that difficult time, we would not have walked in the calling God had and still has for us. Sometimes we must go through difficult times to get to where God wants us to be, both spiritually and geographically.

Yes, there was pain, and I don't wish that on anyone. As Rick Joyner jokingly says, "No pain, no pain," meaning, learn things the easy way, so you also don't have to experience pain later. Some learn differently than others. Some learn the hard way. That was us, unfortunately we learned *through* the pain.

Lastly, when King Nebuchadnezzar ordered Shadrach, Meshach, and Abednego to be thrown into the fiery furnace, there was a fourth man who was seen walking among the flames. The king and officials **"saw in regard to these men**

that the fire had no effect on the bodies of these men nor was the hair of their head singed, nor were their trousers damaged, nor had the smell of fire even come upon them" (Daniel 3:27 NASB).

When we purchased our second home in New Jersey, the smell of smoke was overwhelming. Over the years, we removed all the sheetrock because it retained the smell of smoke. This was a prophetic picture of what God was doing in our lives, so that no one could smell even "the smell of fire" upon us.

Our hope is that those who go through similar trials will have the hope of restoration, that the accomplished work of the crucified Christ will have its full effect on their lives, and that when they share their testimony, they will not have even "the smell of smoke" upon them. Instead, when they go through trials, the bitterness and evil intent will have no effect on their spirits, so they can truly thank God for His goodness in all things. May His grace be sufficient.

I deeply admire how my husband fought to overcome the enemy's plan to destroy his life. Today, Tom is Vice President of Spiritual Services at MorningStar. He has a pastor's heart and the wisdom from above to solve some of the knotty problems that sometimes happen in large ministries, and he has been used mightily to bring hope to many who have lost hope. He is a living epistle of restoration.

14

Restored!

Eighty years, or two-thirds of Moses' life, were spent in preparation. One exercise I like to do with my preaching audiences is to ask them to hold the first two chapters of Exodus in their left hand, and Exodus 3 through Deuteronomy 28 in their right hand and compare. Exodus 1 and 2 represent Moses' years of preparation; Exodus 3 through Deuteronomy 28 represent his ministry. Preparation is at times difficult and seems like it will never end, but we can take comfort in knowing all the necessary ups and downs were designed for us to equip us for the ministries God has called us to do (see I Corinthians 10:6, 11).

In 2003, I arrived at MorningStar, which has since become my primary place of assignment. All those previous years were God preparing me for the tasks I would encounter in my next season. That is not to say that my prior ministry was insignificant, but those years prepared me and gave me the necessary wisdom and experience to deal with the complexities I would later face.

As I transitioned from being a local church pastor to overseeing a network of more than a hundred pastors, my job description changed considerably, and the complexities of issues increased. However, had I not faced many of those same issues and challenges, I would not have been prepared for this new work of ministry. Still, with my new responsibilities, almost from day one, I felt I was in over my head.

Shortly after I arrived at MorningStar, there was a leadership team meeting in which Rick asked for an honest response from everyone in the room. "How many of you feel qualified to do the job that is assigned to you?" He asked. "If you feel qualified, raise your hand." Of the twelve leaders in the room at the time, only one raised his hand, and it was not me. Since I was relativity new on staff, I did not know how to respond. Would I be asked to step down if I answered wrongly? It was an honest response. At least I was in good company with the eleven other leaders who felt they were in over their heads.

Rick's response was stellar, "Well, good! That means all of you will need to lean heavily on the grace of God to do your job. That is right where I want you to be!" The meeting ended.

While we all need to be careful not to extend ourselves beyond our measure of grace, we also need to know God often puts us in places that require us to stretch ourselves beyond our experience. **"Enlarge the place of your tent, and let them stretch out the curtains of your dwellings; do not spare; lengthen your cords, and strengthen your stakes" (Isaiah 54:2).**

What a novel idea to rely on the grace of God to do your job. While MorningStar had existed for a decade, and half the ministry was breaking into new areas of God-ordained responsibilities, all of us had on-the-job training.

I noticed in Moses' ministry, he did not display near the confidence in his first few encounters with Pharaoh that he did after most of the plagues had been released (see Exodus 5:3, 10:16-17). As our experience with God increases, we grow more confident that He is truly with us.

As I became more comfortable in my new assignment, I discovered new and unimaginable areas of ministry opening to me. Some of these responsibilities required traveling and conducting regional meetings in different areas of the country. Before long, this was expanded to include international travel. The MorningStar Fellowship of Ministries grew globally, and as I became acquainted with this fantastic group of people, I became aware of great deposits of untapped Holy Spirit oil among them.

Largely, our pastors were focused on caring for their local flocks. However, not only did they have a pastoral grace, I soon discovered they were also highly prophetic. To tap into this rich oil reserve, which was pretty much on the surface, all we had to do was get them in the same room talking about God.

Thus began our regional prophetic roundtables with gushers upon gushers of prophetic regional insight downloaded to us, though most of those who attended the regional roundtables were not well-known, prophetic people. Then we conducted similar meetings in different nations around the globe. The gifts were likewise stirred, and the result was a rich, flowing anointing. My role, as meeting facilitator, was to keep the group on topic so we could jointly discover what the Lord was saying to that region. And my, oh my, did God show up! Some of what unfolded gave direction to larger segments of the body of Christ or confirmed new direction God was releasing at MorningStar.

The results were very encouraging. Finally, many leaders who were given high-level revelations could release them among people who valued their contributions. We all had a chance to grow in that atmosphere. Almost without anticipation, the Lord showed us His plans for continents. For Europe, there would be a spiritual "D-Day" invasion. There were oppressive forces controlling the spiritual climate, but liberating forces would be mobilized to free those who were spiritually oppressed.

In a prophetic dream about our visit to Ireland, we were told when we disembarked from our plane, we would be met by two men named "Shamus and Gilbert." This was interpreted to mean the spiritual climate over that nation was controlled by "shame and guilt," both demonic strongholds of the Catholic Church, which had dominated this religious institution for centuries. Such divinely orchestrated opportunities took us even to the presidential palace to deliver a prophetic message to the president.

As the years unfolded, we found ourselves in high-level prophetic meetings with many well-known, well-respected leaders in the church today. I now serve as Vice President of Spiritual Services at MorningStar by invitation of Rick Joyner and Chris Reed. What a far cry from "the worst day of my life"!

Little did I realize in those dark days, the Lord was using that season to prepare me for my ultimate assignment, which He created before the foundations of the world. I walked through that heart-breaking loss of my first church, nearly all our finances, my reputation, confidence, and some would say, even my mind. But as I now look back on those days, one word that describes my life today is, "Restored!"

15

Just Get Them Moving

This vision was unique. As I was in that state between asleep and awake, I was captured by the clarity of what I saw, knowing it contained a profound message. Where I was taken in the Spirit was familiar to me because I had been there before while serving as a member of the U.S. Army. Only, in the vision, this scope was much vaster. Only one other time had I experienced a vision as clear or as weighty.

I was taken to a military parade field in Fort Dix, New Jersey. The field was enormous—at least forty football fields long. It was filled with military tents occupied by wounded people moaning from their wounds.

Viewing the field from above, I was transported to the front of the field near the parade stand. As I drew closer to the parade stand, I was approached by the Lord, somehow knowing He was about to speak to me. The Lord's face appeared serious, so I listened intently.

In a direct and serious tone, He said, "I want you to help these." My heart immediately contradicted. I wanted to obey the Lord, but this was not the job I desired. So, I said, "No Lord, I don't want this job." But the Lord persisted, this time with compassion in His voice, "I want you to help these wounded."

I quickly searched my heart and said again, "No Lord, I really don't want this job." But as soon as those words fell from my lips, I regretted them. I saw the Lord's face, and I could tell this grieved Him. So, I immediately said with a sigh, "Okay Lord, I will take this job." As I looked in His eyes, I sensed that I was not the first person to be offered this position, nor was I the first to turn it down. With my affirmative response, the Lord vanished, leaving me alone to assist with this massive group of wounded people.

At first, I was stunned that He left me alone. After regaining my composure, I thought, "What can I do to help this vast army of wounded people?" Somehow, I knew I needed to survey the field to assess the scope of the problem. The first thing I noticed was there were no leaders in the camp; no one was helping the wounded.

The second thing I noticed was a regressive downward spiral among the wounded. Some individuals were only superficially wounded, but because no attention had been given to their wounds, some were becoming affected with gangrene. Those who were severely wounded were dying because no medical care had been given. As I moved from tent to tent, the conditions were the same. Person after person was crying from their wounds. All were complaining, but no one was helping.

So, I looked for the medical tent and quickly found the medical facility. Hope arose in my heart as I drew back the flap of the tent. I thought, surely this was a place where the wounded could get assistance. As I entered the tent, I looked for some medical tools I could use, but to my horror the medical tools were extremely outdated. The tools looked more like weapons of torture than instruments of healing. How could anyone heal with these?

I also noticed the medical tools had not been cleaned in a long time. There was clearly residue from past surgeries on these tools. I could only imagine how many infections would be passed from one patient to another. My conclusion was that no medical assistance could be provided from this aged and dangerous facility.

As I exited the tent, I could sense that same spirit of hopelessness that rested over the entire camp was trying to enter my spirit. I knew I would have to strongly resist this spirit if I were to help anyone. My final observation was that there were no medical personnel in the tent, and I wondered why I had not noticed that before.

Next, I looked to see if there were any established lines of communication between tents, but quickly realized there was none. As I walked through just one side of the camp, I kept searching for any individual who might help me gather more information on the overall scope of the problems I had observed. Sadly, everyone I sought to enlist refused. Then it became apparent to me that there was no rank and file or leadership whatsoever in this camp.

Finally, I constrained one individual to go to the other side of the camp and come back with a report on the current conditions. Yet somehow I knew, even before this reluctant messenger left, that he would report back the same conditions on the other side of the camp. Indeed, his report was dire. The wounded were growing worse. All were focused on their wounds with little hope. The overall prognosis was ominous.

As I considered the weightiness of these conclusions, the dreadful condition of the people, and the overall spirit of hopelessness, my frustration gave way to desperation as I bellowed from the depths of my soul, "Lord, You can't leave me like this!"

With that, the Lord reappeared as quickly as He had departed. I awaited His answer. As I looked at Him, He gestured with His eyes toward a small group of individuals seated in a remote part of the camp. As He gestured, I immediately knew three things: 1) This was not a modern-day army, but a revolutionary army like the one that fought to free America, 2) this small group of individuals seated in the remote part of the camp was a fife and drum corps, and 3) the Lord's answer for these wounded was somehow related to this fife and drum corps.

As the Lord's gaze turned from the fife and drum corps, His eyes fell back on me with clear instructions on what I must do next. He said, "Get the fife and drum corps up and marching." At this point I had no idea why the Lord gave these instructions, but I was somewhat encouraged finally having some clear direction.

I quickly ran over to the fife and drum corps. As I drew closer, I could see they were just as wounded as everyone else in the camp. In fact, they looked much like the image portrayed in Archibald Willard's famous "Spirit of '76'" painting of the American Revolutionary War fife and drum corps.

This small group had blood-stained bandages covering a variety of wounds from previous battles but was still healthy enough to rise and march. So, I approached them without so much as an introduction saying, "You all need to get up and march." My instructions were met with predictable resistance, "You must be kidding. We're too wounded to march." While I could clearly see they were wounded, somehow I knew it was still within their ability to march. So, following the Lord's instruction, I said again with as much encouragement as I could muster, "You need to rise and march."

Still not convinced that they would obey, I could tell there was still some fighting left in this group. So, yet again I urged them saying, "You need to rise and march." At last, they struggled to their feet.

As they arose, their obedience was mingled with complaining. I thought to myself, "This group is pathetic. How can this little group have any positive effect on this massive camp?" Nevertheless, I kept instructing them to move forward and march. As they began to move, it was obvious they were in pain, yet they slowly limped along. What happened next was one of the biggest surprises of my life.

As they moved forward and began to play their instruments, the music was the most melodious I had ever heard. I could not believe that such a glorious sound could come from this small group of wounded soldiers. I was both startled and enthralled by this gloriously unexpected turn of events. Suddenly I understood why this army was portrayed as a revolutionary army. This fight they were in, in which so many were wounded, was a battle for liberty and freedom. This battle was to release an army of people from oppression. Caught in the middle of this battle was a vast group of wounded people.

Then, I noticed another curious thing. As the fife and drum corps moved forward to play their instruments, the pace of their marching gradually improved. As I continued to watch these wounded soldiers move forward, I suddenly realized they were being healed as they moved. As their strength was restored, the volume from their instruments grew louder and louder and began to filter through the camp.

Then, as this glorious music washed over the camp, there began a stirring in the tents. As I looked closer, I could see the wounded being drawn to this music. The sound of liberty and freedom was having a powerful effect on them. One by one, the wounded arose and began to fall behind the fife and drum corps. This was not without its challenges because the wounded needed to work through their pain to do this, but then a pattern began to emerge. As the wounded focused on the sound of liberty and freedom, they focused less and less on their wounds until, falling behind the fife and drum corps, each began to be healed.

Not everyone in the camp responded, but for those who did and were determined to overcome the initial pain, healing came. As more individuals responded to this divine call, the clarity of this vision diminished. The sound of liberty and freedom which now filled the entire camp provided deep healing and hope to those who were wounded. I was then caught back up and carried away.

Today, there is a vast army of God's people who have been wounded, some very painfully, as my story depicts. There are more than eighteen million Christians who no longer connect with local churches, largely because of wounds they have received from churches. Many of these wounded are hesitant to reengage in church life.

I was at this camp. I experienced the feeling of being paralyzed and bewildered by my pain, not knowing from whence my help would come. From this vision, it became evident to me that the Lord's heart was for this company of the wounded. In this vision, the Lord's focus was not on vengeance for those who inflicted pain, but on healing and remobilization of this army of wounded warriors. Remember, the walls of Jerusalem were rebuilt with burnt stones. As we review this encounter, we must know there are ways for healing and remobilization to occur.

The American Revolution was fought for liberty and freedom. Many past church movements did not include an atmosphere of liberty and freedom. The Bible has clear boundaries for believers, but also for movements and denominations. There is a host of church traditions and practices that choke out the freedoms God designed for His people.

The movement in which I was raised elevated these traditions and practices to nearly the same level as Scripture. For example, while the Bible preaches holy moderation in drinking, some movements look down on those who exercise this liberty. Much like the Pharisees before them, they make majors out of minors, while neglecting the weightier matters of the law like justice, mercy, and faith (see Matthew 23:23).

In this vision, the sound of freedom was so appealing, it resulted in reengagement for those who moved toward its sound. As some movements shift away from legalistic practices, many that are wounded need to find a camp where this sound of liberty can be heard. I believe in loyalty, but the time has come and gone where loyalty to a church, movement, or denomination outweighs the need to hear and position ourselves to respond to the sound of liberty. This atmospheric change electrified the camp of the wounded and was key to their healing and remobilization.

I recall a vision Rick Joyner once shared with our congregation after he was very sick with COVID. Rick had determined that while he had suffered great distress from the virus, he would make every effort to raise his voice in thanksgiving to God. Then the Lord showed him a vision of the Father with His head bowed and weeping. He wondered what had caused the Father to weep so profusely. The Lord then explained that it was his worship in his moment of deep distress that touched the heart of the Father and caused Him to weep deeply.

Those who find themselves deeply wounded have great opportunities that do not come along often in our lifetimes. When life's circumstances are adverse and we are going through trials, we have a choice: remain focused on the pain, or with all the strength we can muster, put one foot in front of the other and worship and live to fight another day.

As I write this, I recall the days when my greatest hope was just to make it to noon without giving up. In this vision, those who responded to the music were willing to take those first painful steps which created a surprising army of overcomers. The medical tools were terribly outdated and had not been sanitized in a long time and were likely to cause dangerous, life-threatening infections had they been used.

When the Lord sent us back to New Jersey, our church could have been a case study in how to give proper care and attention to bruised people. Not only were the people wounded, but they had also lost simple trust in leaders to do right before God. When people have a poor experience with a doctor, they are much more careful in choosing their next doctor. It is a delicate road to walk down to regain the trust of people who have had poor past experiences.

The first order of business for any doctor is to have clean hands. As we began to gather the people, we had to carefully communicate that we had no agenda for their lives. In our first public meetings, we made it a point to put no pressure on anyone to attend our gatherings. We said, "If you feel like attending our meetings, we welcome you to attend. If you feel the best thing for you to do on Sunday is to stay home, stay home. If you would like to give offerings, give. If you don't want to give, don't give." These were battle-wounded, scarred, and weary people. We told them we had no expectations other than to provide a place for them to come if they desired to come and interact with other believers. Eventually, after they were healed, they came to every meeting and tithed.

Our ministry was to tend to the bruised and wounded. While we ourselves were in this company, helping others deal with their disillusionment greatly helped us deal with ours. Proverbs 11:25 is most helpful to the bruised: **"The generous soul will be made rich, and he who waters will also be watered himself."** When we, out of our pain, minister to others, we also receive healing.

When this principle is activated in the lives of believers, it becomes key to releasing healing to an entire camp. In time, and with no plan in place, people gradually regained their spiritual traction and trust in leadership. Additional fresh vision, the new thrust of the Toronto Blessing, Rodney Howard Brown's ministry, and MorningStar conferences were all new manna from heaven being poured out like water on the thirsty.

Over the last few decades, I have often reflected on this vision of the fife and drum corps and my assignment to activate those who can pipe out the sound of liberty and freedom. As Director of MorningStar Fellowship of Ministries, I have had opportunities to connect with leaders all over the globe who can release that sound and call the army of God to remobilize.

I have had the privilege of watching leaders light up with great enthusiasm as they watched this army fall into rank. I have led prophetic roundtables in several nations which have altered the spiritual climate and given hope to those who had lost hope. Yet, much work remains, and the best is yet to come!

As I close this chapter, my prayer is that you hear the sound God is releasing today. I am convinced that, from this group of tattered and weary soldiers, there is great richness God wants to release. This group has songs to sing that no one else can sing. My hope is that you will be resolved and motivated to join me in that company of people God has labeled "Restored!"

16

Reflections

As I reflect on my story, it seems like another lifetime. I have learned so much since that "worst day of my life," and have marveled at the unseen hand of God steering my life into unimaginable personal and ministry opportunities.

Some of the most meaningful relationships I have had in the kingdom were with people from churches I started at Trenton Christian Center and LifeSpring, both in Trenton, New Jersey.

As God changed our geography, He expanded our relational connections. As the years unfolded, we became acquainted with many leaders through MorningStar's Fellowship of Ministries. I have come to deeply respect the men and women who stand on the front lines, laying down their lives for God's people. These are genuine servants of God whom I have been privileged to walk alongside for many years. We have laughed and cried together and picked each other up when one of us was down. We have also buried some of God's best and welcomed new and emerging prophetic leaders.

The consistent testimony of our members is their best friends are in our movement. Fred and Donna Hoover, Randy and Dawn Cutter, Tracy Schellhorn, Tom and Jackie Archer, Mike and Roxanne Ginn, and Red and Trish Wilson have been champion elders in MFM and among those with whom we have proudly stood together. At times, I have watched our leaders and ministries receive protection through the counsel and advice of these friends.

Mary Anne and I can say that the advice, love, counsel, and friendships we have received from this group has saved us more than once. The prophetic councils, intercession, and care for one another has touched each member's hearts and God's heart. We have traveled to other nations as teams and watched how God advanced His agenda through this arm of MorningStar. It has been a joy and privilege to see this reality unfold in the Fellowship of Ministries that Rick envisioned from the start.

Some have provided significant prophetic direction for the church today. One prophetic word given to Mary Anne and me at our yearly MFM Retreat was Isaiah 22:22: **"The key of the house of David I will lay on his shoulder; so he shall open, and no one shall shut; and he shall shut, and no one shall open."**

This revealed to us that God would open doors to nations which no man could shut. Soon, effectual international doors began to open to us, and our responsibilities quickly expanded from the U.S. to Europe. We stood amazed as our travels connected us with the "man of peace" in various nations (see Luke 10:6 NASB). These budding relationships had kingdom purposes, which released God-planned deposits into key areas of the world.

One of the most fruitful and enjoyable aspects of my job is to conduct regional and national Prophetic Roundtables. These events are conducted with our local MFM members. One theme that developed during a Prophetic Roundtable in Redding, California, was that the roundtable marked a shift in what God was about to do with MorningStar's prophetic ministry.

The theme of the roundtable was "the barn owl." One of the participants asked if he could share a series of experiences he had had that week. He said twice that week, while walking, he had been attacked by an owl. Then, as he drove to the meeting that morning, that same owl dove toward his car. Among the participants was an ornithologist who studied birds. The ornithologist asked the man, "What color was the owl?" The man answered, "He was white." The ornithologist said, "Well, there are only two owls that are white. One is the snowy owl that lives in the Arctic. The other is the barn owl. This was a barn owl that attacked you."

As we dug deeper, we knew there was a profound interpretation for this. We learned that one distinguishing characteristic of a barn owl is it has a heart-shaped face. Most of us are familiar with eagles as symbols of the prophetic, but God was speaking to us about the barn owl.

And since the barn owl has a heart-shaped face, we concluded that God was telling us the prophetic ministry also has a heart. This was a major word not only for MorningStar, but also for the church at large.

I have since had the privilege of watching the prophetic ministry make this transition, not only at MorningStar, but also throughout the world. For the prophetic ministry to be restored to its respectful place, this heart transformation is critical. Furthermore, I believe the reason God has permitted so many of us to go through heartrending circumstances is to create in us a heart of compassion. God has truly given His called ones a "heart transplant."

I would be remiss not to make note of Mary Anne's and my respect for Rick Joyner. For the past twenty years, it has been our honor and privilege to serve under and alongside Rick. Most established ministries only reach a place of influence after much hard work and sacrifice from their founder. Rick's life has been the epitome of hard work and sacrifice. He is a man of great integrity and worthy to be followed. It has been the honor of our lives to work for this ministry.

We also believe the reason our influence has expanded is because we are working in another man's field (see Luke 16:12). Without exception, in every nation, we were told that Rick Joyner's writings had changed their lives. Rick delegated to us the responsibility of tending to his field of influence. Rick's ministry has indeed expanded into nations. We were simply sent to nurture these developing relationships. For those of us who find ourselves on staff in a large ministry, we must give honor to the pioneering leader who plowed and set the stage for us and for others.

Now the baton at MorningStar has been handed off to Chris Reed. In Chris' first official role at MorningStar, I had a prophetic vision. In it, I saw Columbus' three ships sailing to discover America. From the crow's nests of those ships came the cry, "Land Ho!" And from that moment, new worlds were opened. Today, MorningStar is watching whole new areas of ministry opening to us, and yes, the best is yet to come!

Thirty years later, as Vice President of Spiritual Services at MorningStar, I have been privileged to be a part of many meetings both nationally and internationally with notable, high impact church leaders. I have stood in awe of things I have seen up close and personal as God's miracles have happened. Truly I have been blessed with a wonderful wife who is passionate for the things of God, and I thank God every day for children who love God. I have even had the blessing of holding my children's children in my arms and prayed over them to carry the torch and serve the Lord with all their hearts and all their days. A prayer we often pray for our family is that we would be like Joshua and Caleb, and that the same victorious spirit that was on them would be on our family.

If I may, I would like to share one final word of advice for all those who have walked with us and shared our ups and downs in life's adventure: trust God and enjoy the journey!

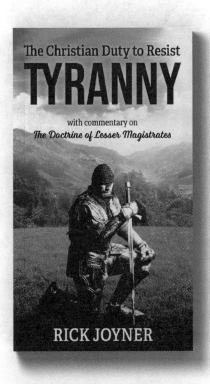

MORNINGSTAR
EVENTS

We pray that each person who attends an event at MorningStar draws closer to God, connects with other believers, and leaves with clarity about their purpose in life.

CHECK OUT OUR UPCOMING CONFERENCES, AND
REGISTER TODAY!

mstarm.org/events